NIVERSI
PN

Schools of Recognition

Schools of Recognition

Identity Politics and Classroom Practices

Charles Bingham

ROWMAN & LITTLEFIELD PUBLISHERS, INC.
Lanham • Boulder • New York • Oxford

ROWMAN & LITTLEFIELD PUBLISHERS, INC.

Published in the United States of America
by Rowman & Littlefield Publishers, Inc.
4720 Boston Way, Lanham, Maryland 20706
www.rowmanlittlefield.com

12 Hid's Copse Road, Cumnor Hill, Oxford OX2 9JJ, England

British Library Cataloging in Publication Information Available

Library of Congress Cataloging-in-Publication Data

Bingham, Charles W. (Charles Wayne)
    Schools of recognition : identity politics and classroom practices / Charles
Bingham.
        p.   cm.
    Includes bibliographical references and index.
    ISBN 0-7425-0195-7 (alk. paper)—ISBN 0-7425-0196-5 (pbk. : alk. paper)
    1. Educational sociology.   2. Social psychology.   3. Recognition
(Philosophy).   4. Identity (Psychology).   5. Social perception.   I. Title.
    LC192.3 .B56 2001
    306.43—dc21   00-066467

Printed in the United States of America

∞ ™ The paper used in this publication meets the minimum requirements of
American National Standard for Information Sciences—Permanence of Paper for
Printed Library Materials, ANSI/NISO Z39.48-1992.

Z1893799

Contents

Acknowledgments

I would like to especially thank Donna Kerr for her intellectual guidance, assuring presence, and philosophical insight during the writing of this work. I am also grateful for the expert readers who gave feedback and insightful criticism on the drafts of these chapters: David Allen, John Stewart, Ed Taylor, Kate Evans, Nick Burbules, and Chris Mayo. I would like to acknowledge the support and teachings of the following cohort of students and professors, who formed an inspiring intellectual community of educators during the time this work was in progress: Remie Calalang, Ellen Timothy, Yoon Pak, Kelly Edwards, Ross Ikawa, Tim Calahan, Sasha Sidorkin, Jaylynne Hutchinson, Kate Evans, and Rosalie Romano. Thanks, too, go to Dean Birkenkamp at Rowman & Littlefield Publishers, whose professionalism and encouragement made the task of bringing this work to published form a pleasure.

1

Introduction: Toward a Framework of Recognition

A CLASSROOM SCENARIO

I begin this work on school recognition with an example from my own life, or maybe I should say from my daughter's life. Being the father of a small child, I often feel that her experience is my own. On Tuesday evening, after Olivia has eaten dinner, she is taken by her mother and me to her first day of Kidsmusic. Olivia is two years old and this is her first classroom experience. We have told Olivia about Kidsmusic beforehand. "Kidsmusic is where there's a teacher, and all sorts of kids, and you get to play music and learn," we explain before class.

At class, Olivia is surrounded by children she does not know. There are parents who speak with their children in ways she is not used to. Some have different accents than Olivia's parents. Some speak more harshly with their children. Some speak with their children very little, some in hushed tones.

And there are other new experiences. She uses instruments—cymbals, sticks, bells, gourds—that are new to her. She is asked to follow the instructions of a teacher she has just met. As these new experiences unfold, Olivia looks more and more at the teacher. The teacher already knows the name of each child, and she calls to Olivia. The teacher asks Olivia if she wants to sing into a small microphone.

Olivia does not go to the microphone to sing. She seems especially shy at this moment. Instead of going to the microphone, she turns to her mother and asks, "Who's *dat?*" She is pointing toward her teacher. Her mother and I are surprised by these words. To begin with, we have never

1

heard our daughter ask "Who's *dat?*" before. It seems like a sophisticated phrase, a phrase that strays from her usual ways of talking. Olivia usually speaks only of needs and demands: "I want . . ." this or that. "Give me . . ." this or that.

It also seems to be a question that is a bit out of context in this situation. We have already told Olivia about listening to the teacher, about doing what the teacher asks. In fact, before the class began, we introduced Olivia to her new teacher. "Olivia," I said, "this is your music teacher, Mrs. Halpern." The answer to "Who's *dat?*" should be obvious to Olivia—it's the teacher we have been preparing her for.

In a sense, the problem of this entire work will be to answer Olivia's question, "Who's *dat?*" Let me explain what I mean. Olivia's question, "Who's *dat?*" can be interpreted in a number of ways. First, it might be said that Olivia is in search of new information. One might say she has arrived at her first day of school and she needs to know some things. She needs to know who this person called her teacher is. She needs to know this to feel at ease. By knowing who this teacher is, she can be more comfortable in her new classroom surroundings.

Another way of interpreting Olivia's question, perhaps a more subtle explanation, might be that she is not actually trying to find out who the teacher is (she has already been told that by her parents, after all), but that she is trying, with her limited vocabulary, to get at something deeper about who *dat* is. Following this second interpretation, we can say she wants to know, in a more general sense, what sort of people teachers are. Perhaps "Who's *dat?*" is a simple way of asking what the role of a person like *dat* is in this new place called a classroom.

There is yet another way of interpreting Olivia's question. This other way explains what I mean when I say that the work of this text is to discuss the implications of Olivia's question. Olivia's question can be interpreted as a matter of *recognition:* she may want to know how she is going to be recognized in this school situation and who she will *be* in this classroom space. Interpreted as a question of recognition, Olivia may be asking "Who does *dat* teacher make *me?*" Understood in this other way, her question is a matter of what happens to a student's identity when she is in this place called a classroom. How does the presence of this new teacher change the way that Olivia looks at herself?

This entire book will, in a sense, look into Olivia's question according to this latter interpretation. This work will examine education through the optic of recognition. It will examine how student self-recognition is affected by teachers, and also how recognition is, in general, affected by school experience. A more general statement of Olivia's question entails the central problem of this work: *What role might recognition play in education?* In this work, I will emphasize recognition as it occurs in educational instances, such as Olivia's first day at school. I argue that questions of recognition are essential to education. We sell education short, just as we sell short Olivia's experience, if we do not consider education in terms of recognition.

What do I mean by recognition? I will begin with a provisional description, given that this work will offer various descriptions of recognitive relations. I hope this provisional description will be looked back upon as inadequate by the end of this work. I take recognition to mean *the act of acknowledging others, and coming to be acknowledged by others.*

Moreover, I would say there are different qualities of recognition. A simple typology for a recognitive event might go something like this: (1) A person can be *recognized*; that is, one can gain acknowledgment that contributes to one's sense of self, and which affirms one's dignity. (2) A person can encounter *nonrecognition*; that is to say, one may find no affirmation. In this case, a person does not "find oneself" during the encounter with the other. (3) A person can suffer *malrecognition* in the sense that one is acknowledged in a way that affronts his or her dignity, or in a way that does not jibe with one's own image of self. The latter two types, nonrecognition and malrecognition, I will lump under the general category of *misrecognition* from now on. Misrecognition, whether it be through an absence of acknowledgment, through negative acknowledgment, or through wrong acknowledgment, is an affront to personal dignity. Misrecognition is the undesirable alternative to recognition. I introduce these broad categories now, though the work of this book will certainly throw into question the lack of nuance entailed in this simple typology.

But why recognition? Why have I chosen to study recognition as an educational concern? Why do I think that my daughter's recognitive experience on her first day of class is educationally significant? My interest in recognition is motivated both by my own experience as a teacher, and also by my reading in philosophy and social theory.

I began my teaching career in a part of the world where the link between recognition and education has long been explicit in some very political ways. Between 1983 and 1987, I taught school in South Africa under the loathsome apartheid regime. As a white person teaching in an all-black school, I learned not only about the devastating educational injustices that were perpetrated by the apartheid government, but I also learned from friends and students about how schools must be a venue for racial and cultural recognition. I heard stories of the 1976 Soweto uprising. When the government was about to insist that students be subjected to the Afrikaans language as a medium of instruction, students boycotted. They demanded that their voices be heard in school. They demanded that the language of Afrikaans, the quintessential language of racist misrecognition, not be used in the classroom. In order to gain recognition, they boycotted schools and made their presence known on the streets. Teaching under the apartheid regime, I learned the important link between recognition and education.

As a teacher in the United States, I have been troubled that there is not such an explicit link between recognition and schools. Such a link is not widespread in current educational discourses. It seems to me that schooling is too often assimilated to issues of course content, teaching methods, and school rules—and that these issues are usually devoid of discussions of human acknowledgment. Take, for example, two former students of mine, junior high school boys whose first language is Spanish. Juan and Charles spent the first half-year of ninth grade speaking Spanish in the hallways, in the parking lot, at the bus stop, anywhere *but* in the homeroom class where I was the teacher. I remember wondering what it was about the space of my classroom that prevented them from feeling comfortable enough to speak their home language in my classroom. One day in January I finally "got a clue" and invited them to feel free to speak Spanish in my classroom. Sure enough, Juan and Charles began, hesitantly for the first few days and then later without inhibition, to converse in Spanish every morning. I was happy about their use of Spanish in my classroom, with only a vague sense of why their speaking Spanish was important. As a teacher, I had never been introduced to a notion of recognition that would enable me to think through this sort of classroom scenario. Now I would say that speaking one's own language in the public space of the classroom indicates that one feels oneself *there,* that one feels acknowledged. Not feeling free to speak one's own language indicates a lack of classroom recognition.

A former student of mine, Patrick, was constantly tormented at school. Patrick was an effeminate ninth-grade boy, and the other ninth-grade boys at school harassed him mercilessly. During a language arts class that I was teaching, another boy, Bill, called Patrick a "faggot," while Patrick sat sullen, quiet, and embarrassed. I became irate and took Bill out into the hall to yell at him, even though I knew at the time how useless my yelling was. Patrick was being misrecognized, being given a demeaning picture of himself, all over campus. He spent lunchtimes alone. Rather than risk being acknowledged negatively, Patrick chose not to be acknowledged at all. Ultimately, Patrick decided to move to a different state to live with his father. He did so, he told me, because he was suffering so much at our school. Patrick was acknowledged in a way that was an affront to his dignity. He was misrecognized.

As I have learned from my teaching experience, and as these examples bear out, schools are places where matters of recognition get played out. The recognitive encounter can be political, as in the Soweto example; it can be cultural, as in the case of Juan and Charles; or it can be personal and psychological, as in the case of Patrick. As I will argue in this work, sometimes the political, the cultural, and the psychological need to be considered in a conversation with each other. Political, cultural, and psychological acknowledgments are intertwined, and they need to be so considered when we think about schools. My experience as a teacher has shown me that recognition is so often at play in schools that it must not be ignored.

While I have long been concerned with issues of recognition in schools, it has not been so long that I have been able to articulate why these issues need to be the focus of an educational study such as this work. That is where my own research in social theory comes into play. I have found a set of discourses that, deriving either directly or indirectly from Hegel's philosophical notion of recognition, help to make sense of the link between recognition and education that I have experienced. Recognition is not only a matter obviously at stake in schools; recognition is also a philosophical notion that has gotten a lot of attention in the works of various social theorists. In the past, the theoretical work on recognition has not been explicitly mapped onto the educational domain. This work is motivated by the need to bring recognitive theory and educational practice together. In joining them, I hope to address the educational implications of the most important recognitive question: How can human dignity be acknowledged again and again?

PAST EDUCATIONAL RESEARCH INTO RECOGNITION

While educational theorists have not taken up the theme of recognition per se, recognition has been implicitly presented in educational theory. In this section, I will go over some important educational discussions that foreshadow this work's attention to recognition. These discussions regard multicultural education, psychoanalytic theories of pedagogy, race identity–development theory, Mike Rose's consideration of "the politics of remediation," and the "ethic of care." In addition to outlining how each of these educational discussions is similar to my study of educational recognition, I will also mention how this study offers insight that goes further than these existing conversations.

Certainly multicultural education is in many ways about student recognition. Perhaps multicultural education, with its roots in prejudice reduction and intergroup education, is the main precursor to any educational study of recognition.[1] As we will see later, Charles Taylor goes so far as to claim that the main purpose of multicultural curriculum reform is to promote recognition of students from diverse backgrounds. I do not claim to be an expert on multicultural education, and I am not presumptuous enough to assimilate multicultural education to recognition as Taylor does. However, I do think that recognition is a useful lens by which to approach multicultural education. Following Taylor's lead, we can learn a few things, as I will point out in the first chapter.

The significant difference between my own study of recognition and a more general argument for multicultural education is that multicultural education does not carry on a sustained discussion of recognition per se. Recognition has not yet been systematically theorized in discussions on multicultural education, whereas recognition has been well theorized in the four Hegelian discourses I will be taking up. As these chapters unfold, we will have opportunities to address the possible intersections between recognition and the aims of multicultural education. Because some aims of multicultural education are very close to the concerns of a project of recognition, these intersections are inevitable.

Recent psychoanalytic studies of pedagogy also foreshadow the present study of recognition. Within the recent educational literature on Freudian psychoanalysis, one common theme that is taken up is the way that knowledge acquisition intersects with the "defenses of the ego."[2] Freudian-minded educators claim that one cannot separate the ego's claim to stability from educational interaction. For example, if a student who is homophobic is asked to learn about lesbian culture, that student may become very defensive about the alleged reasons that she should not have to study lesbian culture. Educational theorists, taking cues from psychoanalysis, have noted that such defensiveness may have more to do with the self of the student than with course content. The content may be rejected out of hand simply because it is a threat to the student's ego identity.

What does such an understanding of psychic resistance have to do with recognition? As I understand this particular Freudian take on learning, the classroom is being posited as a site where identity is at stake—and such a positing comes very close to the notion of recognition. The student's ego identity is actually dependent upon a classroom "struggle." While this understanding of psychic resistance may not be quite as other-dependent as Hegelian recognition, while the threatened ego is a matter more of the "I" alone than another's acknowledgment of the "I," this Freudian understanding of ego defense certainly accentuates the self-as-needful, as does the concept of recognition. In both Freudian pedagogy and education grounded in recognition, the self in the classroom needs positive acknowledgment of who he or she is. The main difference between the two is that in the latter the other takes a more active role in the affirmation of self.

Another precursor to this study of educational recognition is the work on dialogue and racial identity development done by Beverly Tatum.[3] Tatum outlines the various stages of racial identity development. She points out that race identity varies along the following continuum: "Preencounter, Encounter, Immersion/Immersion, Internalization, and Internalization–Commitment."[4] Her aim is to sensitize educators to these various stages. If teachers can keep these stages in mind as they encourage their students to have dialogues on race and racism, if they can actually teach these stages to their students, then students may have an easier time dealing with the uncomfortable feelings that sometimes surround such discussions. For example, if a student can say to herself, "I am having trouble communicating my feelings to this person because I am at the Encounter stage but he is at the Internalization stage," then it may be easier for that student to negotiate conversational uncomfortability. While I do not agree with the reification and normalization of race identity that accompanies Tatum's developmental theory, I do think that Tatum is implicitly addressing an issue of recognition in the classroom. Basically, Tatum is worried that discussions of race and racism in the classroom tend to be struggles for recognition. As such, conversations can break down if recognition is not attained. If my racial identity cannot be recognized, then the conversation cannot continue; but if others can acknowledge the worth of my own identity position, then I will have dignity enough to stay in the conversation. Naming the other by means of assigning to the other a developmental place marker is one way to promote recognition.

Another educational analysis that foreshadows this study is Mike Rose's description of the "politics of remediation." In his *Lives on the Boundary*, Rose takes a provocative look at the instruction of English composition.[5] In his dealings with Suzette, one of his students at a remedial writing center, Rose notes that the quality of Suzette's writing is hampered not so much because she uses improper grammar, and not so much because she uses sentence fragments, though these problems are present in her writing. Instead, Rose notices that her writing succumbs to the expectations that Suzette places on her *self* when she writes. Suzette is convinced that there is a certain way that her writing is supposed to sound because she is a college student. As Suzette explains, she wants to write "the way people write essays in college."[6] As Rose shows, this educational exercise, one that might ordinarily be construed as a matter of the application of grammatical rules, is the site of a struggle for recognition. As Suzette writes, she is struggling with who she is as a college student. She wants not only to be articulate, but she wants to be recognized as a person who is in college, who can do the work of a college student. Through her writing, she wants recognition.

Nel Noddings's work on the ethic of care is another relative of this work. This kinship is most obvious in her text *Caring: A Feminine Approach to Ethics & Moral Education*.[7] The similarities between Noddings's text and this work are twofold. First, both address topics that overlap at least nominally: they investigate Martin Buber's notion of confirmation and the notion of reciprocity. Second, Noddings's text emphasizes interpersonal relationships in much the same way that this work will. Noddings uses human interaction as an organizing principle for thinking about education just as I will be doing. However, this work takes confirmation, reciprocity, and the organizing principle of human interaction in a much different direction than does Noddings's work, which assumes that human caring is a good in itself that needs to be well described and then well practiced. Her aim is to describe an ethical practice of nurturance that others can follow in lieu of following disembodied, rationalistic procedures for solving moral dilemmas. In terms more suited to this work, we might say that Noddings aims to describe the best way to practice recognition. In contrast to Noddings's approach to caring, my approach is not that recognition is one certain thing that we can describe well and then attempt to practice well accordingly. On the contrary, I will argue that recognition has been effectively described in at least four different, and somewhat contradictory, ways. The aim of this work is not to pin down educational recognition and apply it accordingly, but rather to proliferate its possible uses.

ANALYTICAL FRAMEWORK

Each of these precursors to our discussion implicitly takes up the notion that students engage in struggles for recognition in school. The difference between my focus and these precursors is twofold. First of all, in the following chapters we will be dealing with the theme of recognition explicitly. While the human need for recognition is presumed to be at work in various models of education, I think it is important for educators to see such a need in its own right. Second, this work will apply particularly Hegelian understandings of recognition to educational scenarios. As the following chapters will bear out, recent conceptions of recognition that derive either directly or tangentially from the Hegelian conception prove to be useful for an educational analysis. This work differs from its precursors in that it does not take a multicultural, a Freudian, a developmental, a writerly, or a moral proceduralist perspective on recognition.[8] Instead, this work will look into a philosophical understanding of recognition that has its roots in Hegel.

Why distinguish recognition instead of leaving it as an implicit educational concern? This question gets at both the normative grounding of this book and at its usefulness as a mapping of recognitive relations in education. To be sure, this study relies on the normative claim that human beings need something from one another when they come together in places such as schools. Human beings need dignity. It is my claim that dignity is nurtured through recognitive means within human encounters. During the course of this book, when I use terms like "should" and "must" with regard to recognition, I use them because human dignity *must* be nurtured between people. My bottom line is that human beings *need* recognition because they *deserve* dignity.

But the advantage of a recognitive analysis does not rest comfortably in the claim that recognition lays the groundwork for a dignity of relation. As I will argue, recognition is fraught with peril, power, and limitation as well. It is not a simple matter of "We should study recognition because it is a moral good." In many ways, recognition is also *not* a moral good. There are wounds and injuries that quickly become apparent when recognition is subject to analysis. For example, and this will be a theme that is given closer scrutiny in the chapters that follow, much recognition of racial identity is infected with racist histories that cannot be completely avoided in the racist matrix of modern/postmodern culture. Much recognition of homosexual identity is similarly infected with heterosexist histories that run unchecked in this postmodern world. Dealing with and identifying recognition is thus also necessary in order to begin parsing the complex activity, both the good and the bad, that leads to intersubjective dignity. I must also categorize the dangers and drawbacks of recognition—the recognitive scenarios that lead to misrecognition, malrecognition, and nonrecognition.

In addition to these normative concerns, studying recognition in education is very practical. Recognition, as it has been articulated in its various twentieth-century manifestations, proves to be a flexible language for speaking to human dignity in education. Recognition is helpful for rethinking significant educational concerns such as the school as a public space and transformative curriculum, as well as teacher–student and student–student relationships. Recent conceptions of recognition, conceptions that derive either directly or obliquely from the Hegelian notion, are educative with regard to education. To borrow a phrase from pragmatist philosopher William James, recognition, explicitly described, is an "idea upon which we can ride."[9] Some of the more specific questions of recognition with which I will deal are offered in the next section.

Objectives: Educational Questions This Work Will Address

While I have spoken so far to recognition in general, the aim of this work is to address four specific educational questions that the notion of recognition brings into focus:

- In what would attending to student recognition in the distinctly public space of the school consist?
- Must the other be knowable in order to be recognized?
- If some sense of recognition entails subjection, can classroom recognition still contribute to one's dignity?
- What would reciprocal recognition look like in educational settings?

The method of this work is philosophical and pragmatic. The concept of recognition I take as a point of departure has its origins in philosophy. The normative claims of this work are pragmatic insofar as I am concerned with showing that the concept of recognition has a lot of use value in the field of education.

My analysis of recognition derives from the philosophy of G. W. F. Hegel, but I do not claim him as a stable philosophical figure. In this way, my reading is different from that of those who want to interpret Hegel in one certain way. I regard Hegel as the founder of a philosophical discourse on recognition that has continued into this century. Describing the founders of discourses—thinkers such as Nietzsche, Freud, and Marx— Michel Foucault says this:

> In a somewhat arbitrary way we shall call those who belong in this last group "founders of discursivity." They are unique in that they are not just the authors of their own works. They have produced something else: the possibilities and the rules for the formation of other texts.[10]

Foucault's argument with regard to discourses is that philosophy is best construed not as a disciplinary pursuit that is limited by the opus of this or that philosopher; rather, philosophy should be considered as the pursuit of discourses that take the author's work more as a point of departure than as a limitation. For example, the concept of recognition originated in the domain of philosophy, but modern texts on recognition are what Foucault calls "transdiscursive." The philosophical discourse on recognition has found its way into political theory, Jewish existentialism, feminism, and psychoanalysis. This work is philosophical in Foucault's discursive sense. I will track the philosophical notion of recognition through these four recent manifestations.

Moreover, pragmatist philosophy enlightens my normative claims. As I have mentioned, I aim to show that the philosophical notion of recognition inaugurates a useful discourse for examining education. Claiming that it is a useful discourse is different from other sorts of claims. I do not claim to prove that human recognition is, in itself, a moral good. Nor do I claim to show what educational recognition is, especially since the versions of recognition I study sometimes contradict each other. I do not claim to prove, in general, that schools either do or do not promote recognition, although I will claim that recognition needs to be attended to in schools. My claim is quintessentially pragmatic insofar as I will show that the concept of recognition is useful for education. Following John Dewey's definition of a normative principle as "a tool for analyzing a special situation," I claim in this work that educational recognition is a moral good because it is an instrument of consequence.[11] I will describe four conceptions of recognition, which together make up a lexicon for thinking about what students, teachers, curricula, and schools do. The pragmatic aim of this work is to construct a workable language out of the raw discursive material of recognition and then to use that language to think about the classroom. If this recognitive language is useful, if it helps us to effectively analyze some current concerns in education, then my pragmatic aim will have been achieved.

By saying that I will establish a lexicon for the notion of recognition, I do not claim to be making some dispassionate overview of the possible ways that recognition can be described. Establishing such an overview would mean that one surveys all or most of the various descriptions of a topic, and that one does so with the confidence that the topic itself survives in spite of its descriptions. First of all, I do not claim that this book's lexicon is in any way exhaustive. The four theorists who are addressed in this book are not the only ones who have worked within recognitive terrain; to act as if these four perspectives were somehow exhaustive, or even representative, of what can be said about recognition would be misleading. The four perspectives that will form the recognitive vocabulary of this book are but a snippet of the ways recognition might be described. However, I do maintain that they make up an important snippet, full of import for educational thought.

Second, I cannot make a dispassionate overview precisely because I do not believe that recognition is any one particular thing that can stand aside from the vocabularies that bring it into existence. I do not believe that there is some thing-in-itself called recognition that can be described more or less precisely by this or that description. On the contrary, I take the standpoint that recognition is completely entwined with how we describe it. When I use four different ways of describing recognition, I am not trying to give an overview that claims to describe what recognition really is. I am rather trying to push recognitive sensibilities into educational thought through various descriptions that offer different ways that recognition might be understood.

What I am trying to do with these alternative vocabularies of recognition is not based on overview of the topic, but rather on differing perspectives of recognition. We only have perspectives when it comes to engaging our world. A hand, or a cigar, or a smile is fully determined by the perspective that we bring to understanding it. When I think of a smile, I cannot hope to get at some true essence of that smile beyond what my perspective allows me to grasp. If my perspective tells me that the smile is aimed to deceive, then the truth of that smile is that it is aimed to deceive—unless I can open myself to understanding some new perspective. Another perspective might be that the smile depicts happiness, in which case I will engage with that smile accordingly. Whether I engage with that smile as an act of deception or happiness depends completely upon the perspective that I take up at the point of engagement. I may not actually know which is the "correct" perspective when it comes to a particular smile, but the point is not to get at the "correct" perspective.

The point is—and this goes for recognition as well as for smiles—that it is more advantageous to be able to jump from one perspective to another than to be stuck in only one perspective. Whereas an overview attempts to survey the various possible interpretations of a given scenario in order to adjudicate between them, a perspective-based analysis claims that more than one perspective on an event, even if those perspectives disagree with one another, is always more preferable than a singular viewpoint. It is useful to have an arsenal of perspectives.

Utilizing the Hegelian notion of recognition in conjunction with contemporary theory, this analytical framework is organized around the four educational questions I described earlier.

Hegel's conception of recognition was laid out during his early Jena writings.[12] With his notion of recognition, Hegel addresses at least four questions. The first is this: How does the modern person attain recognition in the public sphere? Second, Hegel asks: How can I recognize an other when the other is in fact independent of me? Third: What can I do if recognition of me is already a matter of subjection? And fourth: What would reciprocity look like within the event of recognition?

In this section, I will illustrate that these questions, while indeed being related to each other because they are motivated by problems inherent to Hegel's analysis of recognition, are fruitfully investigated in very different discourse communities. These four questions of recognition have been usefully appropriated by Charles Taylor, Martin Buber, Judith Butler, and Jessica Benjamin respectively. Clearly, these thinkers, coming from different discourse communities, have diverse orientations. Taylor is a theorist of political liberalism, Buber is a theorist of Jewish existentialism, Butler comes from a poststructuralist perspective, and Benjamin works within a psychoanalytic tradition. The questions that Hegel was struggling with in his articulation of recognition were diverse questions that are best taken up under different discursive assumptions. In the concluding chapter, I will expand on the way that the different discursive assumptions serve recognition usefully under different circumstances. For now, let an analogy suffice. At different times, physicists use two different models to describe the movement of light: the particle model and the wave model. Quite simply, these models are incommensurate yet are both applicable. That is how I find it with different models of recognition. They are at the same time incommensurate and applicable. Hegel asks four very different questions whose problematics are best pursued in diverse discourse communities.

Recognition and Public Dignity: Mirroring

I begin with a conception of public recognition that Charles Taylor has emphasized. This conception has to do with recognition outside of one's home. In his Jena period, Hegel grapples with this question: How does the individual attain recognition in the public sphere?[13] He limns a private/public understanding of the individual's need for recognition. The individual progresses through three domains in which her need for recognition must be met. The first domain is private, while the last two are public. The individual progresses from the private family to the public domains of civil society and the state. In the first domain, the bourgeois family, Hegel describes bonds with loved ones as already recognitive insofar as love bonds require mutuality between self and other. Hegel describes the love between husband and wife as an exemplary instance of mutual recognition: "Love is recognition without conflict of will."[14] In love, "each is herself/himself in the being-for-self (Fursichsein) of the other . . . each is conscious of being-for-self in his/her singularity in the consciousness of the other."[15] Family bonds are envisioned by Hegel as a distortion-free version of recognition at work. For Hegel, recognition is immediately present at home because love proceeds by means of distortion-free recognition. According to Hegel, no mediation is needed between self and other in the private domain. Self–other mutuality is what the private sphere is based on.

The public domain, as it is conceptualized by Hegel, is different in kin but not in kind from the private domain. Just as the individual needs recognition at home, so too she needs recognition in public, that is, in civil society and in the state. But in the public domain, recognition cannot be taken for granted as it was in the private domain of the family. As diverse individuals bump up against others whom they do not know, recognition will not be easily granted. There will be struggles for recognition. Hegel maintains that many public struggles are best understood in terms of the individual's need for recognition. For example, if one person steals property from another, Hegel would have us understand that the owner of the property will seek retribution not only because she wants her property back, but also because she wants recognition as the owner of that property. In other words, a struggle about my property is fundamentally a struggle about *who I am*. Laws are established not only to protect one's goods, but they are established also to guarantee the recognition of the person who is involved in a legal struggle.

Charles Taylor takes this Hegelian question about public recognition and maps it onto the current debate over multiculturalism. He uses a recognitive lens to explain why societies must enact laws that recognize various social groups. Using the same liberal framework that Hegel employed, he distinguishes between the private and public domains while maintaining that each of these domains needs to be a site of recognition. Taylor explains the private/public split as follows:

> recognition has become familiar to us, on two levels: first, in the intimate sphere, where we understand the formation of identity and the self as taking place in a continuing dialogue and struggle with significant others.[16] And then in the public sphere, where a politics of equal recognition has come to play a bigger and bigger role.[17]
>
> Indisputably, more and more societies today are turning out to be multicultural, in the sense of including more than one cultural community that wants to survive. The rigidities of procedural liberalism may rapidly become impractical in tomorrow's world.[18]

According to Taylor, modern societies need a recognitive liberalism. They need a liberalism that is prepared to recognize the dignity of each individual when he or she is in the public domain. The dignity of the public person can best be recognized by recognizing the cultural community to which that person belongs. According to Taylor, multicultural societies need to mirror back, in a positive way, the cultural communities of diverse individuals.

Taylor takes as his example the Canadian discussion over Quebec separatism. He says that the Hegelian understanding of a struggle for recognition offers a useful means by which to understand the need for a distinct society of French-speaking Quebec citizens. Quebeckers, he argues, need to have their culture recognized. In a very real sense, Quebeckers are in a life-and-death struggle since their culture may not survive if assimilation sets in. Their struggle is about who Quebeckers are; it is about each Quebecker's dignity. Taylor argues that Quebeckers need to see and hear their francophone culture not just at home but in the public sphere as well. Laws that preserve a sense of that francophone culture in the public domain will contribute to the dignity of each Quebecker. Such laws will create space for public recognition by providing a public mirror for the Quebec individual.

In sum, Charles Taylor teases out the contemporary political implications of Hegel's recognitive liberalism. Taylor considers the same question that Hegel addressed: How does the individual attain dignity in the public sphere? As Taylor explains, contemporary multicultural societies are working out an answer to this question. Individuals can attain dignity through a positive mirroring of their cultural communities. A person needs cultural recognition. Because liberalism is marked by an ongoing concern for the private/public split, this question is best pursued within the discourse community of political liberalism. Charles Taylor makes good use of Hegel's question within that arena of thought. As the next section will show, Hegel's second recognitive question does not similarly lend itself to liberal thought.

Recognition of the Independent, Unknowable Other: Confirmation

Martin Buber has given extended consideration to a second question that is lodged within Hegel's presentation of recognition: How can I recognize an other when the other is in fact independent of me? This specific question already assumes a certain standpoint with regard to a larger configuration of questions about how the self is related to others. Larger questions are: Was Descartes correct to assume that the human self is self-contained? Or, is the human self-constituted through an intersubjective process? If human selves are intersubjective, does that mean that we share a commonality? Hegel's presentation of recognition in the *Phenomenology of Spirit* assumes two things with regard to these larger questions. First, the self is an intersubjective self that needs recognition; and second, although self and other partake in intersubjective recognition, they nevertheless remain autonomous selves. Hegel is concerned with how recognition happens given these two broad assumptions.

In the *Phenomenology*, Hegel describes, in very compact and complex terms, the succession of steps that recognition follows. These steps include a solution to the problem of recognizing an other who is initially independent, and who remains independent, in spite of intersubjective recognition. Let me give a simplified version of these steps. First, explains Hegel, "Self-consciousness is faced by another self-consciousness; it has come *out of itself*."[19] The self, in the process of recognition, confronts an other and then takes the other over in order to eliminate the problem of otherness. The self seeks to see the other on the self's own terms. According to Hegel, the self begins by colonizing the other. This initial coming-out-of-oneself is derivative because the self, as Hegel says, "does not see the other as an essential being, but in the other sees its own self."[20] By joining with the other, the self negates the specific otherness of the other. Such a union foils the initial aim of recognizing an other since this union suppresses otherness into sameness. The next step is then for the self to cancel out the other-as-self in order both to get the self back on its own terms and to give the other back on its own terms. The self "cancels its being in the other [*sein Sein im Andern*], and lets the other go free."[21] Through a self-cancellation and a giving-back of the other, both self and other retain independence. The steps of recognizing an independent other are now complete.

Martin Buber struggles with this very same Hegelian question of how to recognize an other who is independent of me, but Buber takes Hegel's question into territory that is much less abstract. He wants to know how, in the time of human meeting, I can confirm an other even though that other is quite independent of me. Before I look into how Buber attempts to deal with Hegel's second question, I want to note the existential bent of Hegel's steps to recognition. Questions, like Hegel's second, of self and other find voice within the existential tradition. When Buber addresses the concern of Hegel's second question, he too speaks in an existential vocabulary. Hegel's second question finds its home in a different discourse community than his first question. Worrying about the lived process of intersubjective recognition has little to do with thinking about the private/public split.

With his notion of confirmation, Buber grapples with the problem of how I come to recognize an other who is independent of me. Albeit without direct admission of a debt to Hegel, Buber takes Hegel's second question and maps it onto the experience of human meeting when one person wants to confirm an other.[22] Buber points out, along with Hegel, that confirming an other will be derivative if I confirm the other in my own image. I must be able to confirm an other person as independent and other. Writes Buber,

> The basis of man's life is twofold, and it is one—the wish of every man to be confirmed as what he is, even as what he can become, by men; and the innate capacity in man to confirm his fellow men in this way.[23]

Buber's account of confirming an other in all her otherness shares with Hegel a concern that we must not colonize the other. The other must not be reduced to me. If I am to confirm an other, I must confirm her as *not I*.

Buber's solution to the problem of confirming an independent other is different from Hegel's. For Buber, I needn't go through a struggle of dominating the other and then releasing her. Instead, I can avoid this struggle by preparing beforehand for the confirming situation; or rather, I can prepare beforehand by not preparing beforehand. I can prepare for the other by acknowledging that the other is apt to take me by surprise. I should realize that confirmation would require letting the other happen to me in a way that I cannot anticipate.[24] As Buber explains,

> In spite of all similarities every living situation has, like a newborn child, a new face, that has never been before and will never come again. It demands of you a reaction which cannot be prepared beforehand.[25]

I not only have the cognitive ability to understand another person from my own point of view, I also have the ontological capacity to let an other take me by surprise and to confirm her as a unique person whom I really don't understand. I would say that Buber's different solution to Hegel's second question is both more reasonable and more applicable than Hegel's own version of "canceling" the other. From within the discourse community of existentialism, Buber has been able to clarify and explicate Hegel's question about recognizing an independent, and in fact unknowable, other.

Let me note the difference between my reading of Martin Buber and a more general postmodern critique of absolute otherness. By highlighting Buber's break with Hegel around the question of confirming independence and unknowability, it might seem that I have linked Buber to the postmodern rejection of dialectic so prevalent in folks like Derrida, Deleuze and Guatarri, and Foucault. Like these and other postmodernists, it might be argued, Buber insists that the other is one more source of incommensurable difference, of non-sameness that slips away from second-order authentication in much the same way that human identity, according to Foucault's discursive understanding, is always based somewhere else than in the concrete experience of a present other. It might be argued that Buber is not within the metaphysics of presence because he conceptualizes the other as absolutely unknowable.

This would be a shallow reading of Buber, and one that I do not embrace, for above all, Buber is a philosopher of presence and a practitioner of existential humanism. Buber's project of confirmation is not meant to unravel the other as such, nor is it meant to unravel the intersubjective project of presence with the other. It is rather meant to teach human beings how to treat the other. Buber's insistence that we treat the other as independent and unknowable is squarely within the modernist tradition of presence-with-an-other. The confirmative project breaks with the Hegelian tendency to dominate the other during such presence, but it does not question presence per se. For Buber, the unknowability of the other is not a dialectical stage to be overcome through progress, nor is it an infection that bars presence. It is a human quality to be embraced through the act of confirmation.

Recognition and Subjection: Discursive Identity

In the *Master and Slave* section of the *Phenomenology*, Hegel takes up his third question: To what extent is recognition of me already a matter of subjection? That Hegel is concerned with this question becomes clear when, in the fourth section of the *Phenomenology*, he moves from an abstract description of the steps involved in a struggle for recognition to a more concrete description of the Master and Slave relationship.[26] The Master/Slave relation comes about because of subjection. In Hegel's concrete description, negation of the other is not as simple as we saw in the previous account. In the Master/Slave situation, the self cannot simply "cancel its being in the other, and [let] the other go free," as Hegel had put it earlier.[27] Instead, negation becomes an actual life-and-death struggle. As I attempt to kill the other, there is a good chance I will not win the battle. But before I lose my very life, I will decide to abdicate. I will assume a position of subjection instead of being killed. Part of the recognitive process involves living with imbalance. As Robert Williams explains the Master/Slave situation,

> One side discovers that the life it is about to lose is as essential to it as the need for recognition. It prefers bare survival to annihilation. . . . It has its existence only at the sufferance of and in dependence on the other. It becomes slave.[28]

Inherent in my struggle for recognition may be that I undergo subjection.

Judith Butler considers Hegel's third question seriously. She addresses this Hegelian problem of subjection from within the intersecting discourse communities of poststructuralism and feminism. She speaks to Hegel's question as it relates to identity. For Butler, identity per se is best understood as a state of subjection. How one is recognized is always a result of the discourses available in culture at large. There is no authentic identity that is just waiting to be recognized; rather, identity is recognized to the extent that it is intelligible. When I seek recognition, I have already agreed to a state of subjection because the terms by which I can be recognized at all are set in advance by the discourses available to the one-recognizing. Recognition is not an acknowledgment of some autonomous core self; it is rather a matter of negotiating for suitable food at the table of discourse. Butler's version of subjection is a discursive one. Being recognized means submitting to discursive codes of intelligibility.

Butler looks, in particular, at the relation between gender identity and Hegel's third question. In her notion of gender discursivity, Butler deals with this question of subjection. Gender identity is discursive in the sense that it only exists as a performance of cultural cues that are already understandable. Thus, if I want to be recognized as a man, I can only be so recognized by submitting to the cultural cues that define manhood. I have no core manhood that resides in me, only to be recognized subsequently. Instead, recognition of me-as-man will be a matter of my being assigned those masculine attributes that are already circulating in culture at large. Butler notes that gender "might be reconceived as a personal/cultural history of received meanings subject to a set of imitative practices which refer laterally to other imitations."[29] Recognition of my identity as male entails my own subjection. Me-as-man does not exist as a core self recognized, but as an identity that is predefined even before the event of recognition.

By focusing on subjection, Butler recommends that humanistic identity politics like those that Taylor advocates be blind to the received history of cultural meanings. Butler may not like the notion of subjection, but she warns that we lose out on political opportunities if we ignore this important matter. Attention to subjection allows us to take our eyes off a false notion of a core self that has essential attributes, such as gender and sexuality, and to pay more attention to the ubiquitous discursive regime by which the very terms of recognition are made possible. Butler's use of Hegel's third question is made possible by an intersection of poststructuralist and feminist sensibilities.

Recognition and Reciprocity

Jessica Benjamin, in her psychoanalytic work, has taken up Hegel's fourth question: What would reciprocity look like within the event of recognition? In Hegel's *Phenomenology*, it is clear that reciprocity hinges on whether the other can simultaneously be an object of my recognition and a subject in her own right. During the event of recognition, there is bound to be an imbalance. If I recognize an other, am I not bound to objectify that other? Isn't there a temptation to consider the other as somehow diminished, since I am, after all, in the position of granting (or withholding) the recognition that the other needs in order to flourish? How then can reciprocity exist? Hegel's fourth question is based upon the dichotomy between the inner self and the outside world. When I recognize an other, there is a qualitative difference between my own inner experience of that other and her own existence per se. It is difficult to know whether my recognition of an other enables us to have a reciprocal relationship, because it is difficult to know if my own conception of the other is in sync with how that other perceives herself.

Hegel answers this question by making the event of recognition into a double bind. He describes recognition in such a way that it cannot happen unilaterally. Recognition always, as Hegel describes it, *already* entails reciprocity. Hegel writes,

> The first does not have a merely passive object before it as in the case of desire. Rather the other is an independent being existing for itself. Consequently the first may not use the other for its own ends, unless the other does *for itself* what the first does. The movement [of recognition] is therefore without qualification the doubled movement of both self-consciousnesses.[30]

In other words, the very process of recognizing an other as a truly independent self in his or her own right means learning that the other is also in a position to recognize me. I can recognize an other only if he or she can also recognize me. Hegel claims that recognition takes place in circuits or it doesn't take place at all. As he puts it, "A one-sided action would be useless, since what is supposed to happen can only come about through the joint action of both."[31] Reciprocity is simply not at stake, because recognition *requires* reciprocity. The problem with Hegel's account of reciprocity is that it is not very convincing; it seems to come by dialectic fiat.

Benjamin, like Hegel, speaks to the question of reciprocity. She too is concerned about how reciprocity is to be achieved during the event of recognition. Benjamin answers this fourth question about reciprocity in a much more specific way than does Hegel. She focuses specifically on the crucial distinction between inner self and outer reality in order to speak to Hegel's question. She does so by taking Hegel's fourth question about reciprocity and fitting it into the logic of psychoanalysis. Such a logic is quite used to talking about the self in terms of its inner and outer reality. For Benjamin, the question of reciprocity must be grappled with in terms of the inner self and outer reality, that is to say, in terms of intrapsychic and intersubjective experiences.

Let us start by looking into Benjamin's understanding of recognition and then move on to how she answers the question about reciprocity. Benjamin argues that the Hegelian event of recognition is best understood in terms of the intersection between the domain of fantasy and the domain of reality. Recognition happens on the fault line between these two domains. I can be recognized by an other only when I acknowledge that the other has an existence that is beyond the control of my own psychic manipulation. Only when I acknowledge the other as an independent subject can the other be autonomous enough to give me recognition that counts. Such recognition depends upon a transition: the other is first within my control, and then I acknowledge that he is outside of my control. Recognition takes place as that threshold is crossed. According to Benjamin, it is the presence of the psyche that makes this crossing available. The fault line between psyche and reality serves as a kind of switchboard through which I can balance my own understanding of the other with the other's independence. While I may, for the most part, consider the other from my own point of view, I cannot gain recognition until the other proves to be greater than an object of my own intrapsychic manipulation. Recognition of me only occurs as the other proves to be a center of existence all his own.

Where does reciprocity come in? Because of psychic life, reciprocity is also possible: I can recognize an other who also recognizes me. Double recognition is the essence of reciprocity. Reciprocity for Benjamin comes from the fault-line tension of recognizing the other who recognizes me. There is a tension involved here because it is tempting to hold the other in the stagnation of fantasy. It feels better to be comfortable with my own understandings of the other. It feels better if the other stays the same, but as Benjamin points out, the switchboard psyche (my phrase) allows the self to tolerate such a tension. The intersection of intrapsychic and inter-subjective experience allows both sameness and difference to exist at the same time. That is to say, the psyche is itself a register that harbors same-ness in the form of intrapsychic representations of the other that are sta-ble, while intersubjective experience of the other is always a matter of life and flux. Benjamin argues that her version of psychoanalytic theory shows how "sameness and difference exist simultaneously in mutual rec-ognition."[32] The other can exist both as object and as subject because human beings have two registers in which to account for the other, a psy-chic register and an intersubjective one. According to Benjamin, mutual-ity and reciprocity are available because the self has a double domain. Jessica Benjamin takes up the tools of psychoanalysis to show how reci-procity works. Working within the contemporary discourse community of psychoanalysis, she notes that our capacity for reciprocity is facilitated by the double register of intrapsychic and intersubjective life.

My agenda in this work will consist of using the analytic frameworks that I have just mapped out to shed light on classroom encounters be-tween self and other, and not to provide a linear argument for a specific educational intervention. It is rather to demonstrate that this analytic framework of recognition can offer insights into how self and other can be positively acknowledged in schools. These four versions of recognition shed light on current concerns in education, such as the public nature of school, curriculum transformation, and self–other interaction in schools. Employing four descriptions of recognition, I argue that schools are places of recognition and that educators must consider schools as such a place if human dignity is to be tended to therein. My agenda is to eluci-date classroom encounters where human dignity is always at stake; such an elucidation is made possible by this work's recognitive framework.

This book will introduce recognitive discourses into education. This goal relates back to the perspectives that are at play as this work progresses, for there will be times when the theorists who talk together in this book are at odds with one another. When I offer various descriptions of recognition, I do not mean to be getting a better handle on one steadfast thing recognition *is*. There is no reality of recognition other than how we describe it. I am intentionally introducing disparate understandings of recognition so that readers of this text can try on multiple recognitive lenses. Some readers will certainly take a deep look at the grounding of these lenses, at the well-rehearsed discursive squabbles that prove, for example, how a psychoanalytic perspective is clearly at odds with recognitive liberalism. Some will argue that a psychic understanding cannot reside happily in a book that also hosts Hegelian historicism such as Charles Taylor's, and that one must adjudicate between them in order to make the book's thinking less fuzzy. To this sort of argument, I can only say that it picks my book up by the wrong handle. I am not trying to argue about which is the best and most accurate framework of recognition; that would be another book. I am rather trying to introduce recognitive thinking, in some of its various iterations, into the realm of education.

The final argument of this work will no longer rely on Hegel. While each of our four relational conceptions of the self–other encounter can be linked to Hegel's notion of recognition, it is not strictly Hegel's model of recognition that will guide this work. It is rather the discourses that have been made possible by Hegel's originary project of recognition. Our four interlocutors do owe some debt to Hegel, but in the rest of this work I will look forward instead of backward. Hegel will be referred to, from here on out, only if his work seems directly useful.

The following chapters will weave the warp of our analytic framework against the weft of school experience. While this chapter has laid out four descriptions of recognitive relations, the following chapters will expand on these descriptions and use them to make sense of how dignity is negotiated between self and other in schools. Chapter 2 will examine Charles Taylor's liberal conception of recognition in light of the work of novelist James Weldon Johnson and postcolonial theorist Franz Fanon. Chapter 3 will examine Martin Buber's relational understanding of confirming the other in all of her otherness. Buber's description of the encounter is useful for thinking about the human acknowledgment of an other who is loathsome or unfathomable, but as novelist Ernest Gaines also brings to light, an educational project of confirmation can also make us cognizant of racism's pervasiveness. Chapter 4 looks at Butler's poststructuralist description of subjection. Using a classroom example of a teacher coming out to her students, I illustrate that the discursive limits of recognition must be taken into account. In chapter 5, I show how relational reciprocity can be understood in terms of intersubjective psychoanalysis. Utilizing the poetry of Langston Hughes, I show how recognition is an active practice as well as a passive act of being acknowledged. Also, I point to educational discourses and institutional practices that must be significantly reconfigured if reciprocity is to be practiced. Chapter 6 puts these four descriptions of the encounter into conversation with one another, as I highlight some of the more important insights that each description offers. Using the recent media reception of the children's book *Nappy Hair*, I provide a case study of a classroom encounter in light of our recognitive discourses.

A comment on how to read the rest of this book is in order. You will notice that the movement of each chapter goes from explanation to critique. That is to say, first a theoretical discourse is enumerated and then specific institutional, societal, and oppressive intrusions into that discourse are investigated. Given that this work is set up to introduce as well as analyze along recognitive lines, I found this sort of movement inevitable. However, this movement is not meant to imply that the power-laden aspects of recognition are somehow secondary. I would thus encourage the reader not to assume that I am arguing for a bland and naïve conception of recognition simply because the more critical stance falls at the end of each chapter. This book is both about theoretical conceptions of recognition and about social critique. I simply could not find a way to insert the latter without establishing the former. It is appropriate to read the rest of this book as if the last part of each chapter matters the most.

NOTES

1. The multicultural education I have in mind is the one described in these texts: James A. Banks, *An Introduction to Multicultural Education* (Boston: Allyn and Bacon, 1994); James A. Banks, "Multicultural Education and Curriculum Transformation," *Journal of Negro Education* 64 (1995): 390–400; James A. Banks, "Transformative Knowledge, Curriculum Reform, and Action," in *Multicultural Education, Transformative Knowledge, and Action: Historical and Contemporary Perspectives*, edited by James A. Banks (New York: Teachers College Press, 1996), 335–348.

2. Here, I am following the work of Alice J. Pitt, "Fantasizing Women in the

Women's Studies Classroom: Toward a Symptomatic Reading of Negation," *Journal of Curriculum Theorizing* 12 (1996): 32–40; Deborah P. Britzman and Alice J. Pitt, "Pedagogy and Transference: Casting the Past of Learning into the Presence of Teaching," *Theory into Practice* 35 (1996): 117–123; Deborah P. Britzman, *Lost Subjects, Contested Objects: Toward a Psychoanalytic Inquiry of Learning* (Albany: SUNY Press, 1999); Elizabeth Ellsworth, *Teaching Positions: Difference, Pedagogy, and the Power of Address* (New York: Teachers College Press, 1997). While much of psychoanalysis might be considered relevant to education, these works make that link explicit.

3. See Beverly Tatum, "Talking about Race, Learning about Racism: The Application of Racial Identity Development Theory in the Classroom," *Harvard Educational Review* 62 (1992): 1–24; Beverly Tatum, *"Why Are All the Black Kids Sitting Together in the Cafeteria?" And Other Conversations about Race: A Psychologist Explains the Development of Racial Identity* (New York: Basic, 1997).

4. Tatum, "Talking about Race," 10.

5. Mike Rose, *Lives on the Boundary* (New York: Penguin, 1989).

6. Rose, *Lives on the Boundary,* 171.

7. Nel Noddings, *Caring: A Feminine Approach to Ethics & Moral Education* (Berkeley: University of California Press, 1984).

8. While the first chapter on mirror recognition and the fifth chapter on reciprocity will take up psychoanalytic notions of recognition, they will be directly informed by Jacques Lacan and Jessica Benjamin, who are particularly Hegelian in their understanding of the psyche. I have used the term "Freudian" in this introduction to distinguish a more strictly psychoanalytic line of thought from the more philosophical (Hegelian) approaches used by Lacan and Benjamin.

9. William James, *Essays in Pragmatism* (New York: Hafner Publishing, 1948), 148.

10. Michel Foucault, "What Is an Author?" in *The Foucault Reader*, edited by Paul Rabinow (New York: Pantheon, 1984), 101–120.

11. Quoted in James Campbell, *Understanding John Dewey* (Chicago: Open Court, 1995), 118.

12. For texts that address recognition and Hegel's Jena period, see especially Robert R. Williams, *Hegel's Ethics of Recognition* (Berkeley: University of California Press, 1997); Robert. R. Williams, *Recognition: Fichte and Hegel on the Other* (Albany: SUNY Press, 1992); and Axel Honneth, *The Struggle for Recognition: The Moral Grammar of Social Conflicts* (Cambridge: Polity Press, 1995).

13. See especially Hegel's *System of Ethical Life* in G. W. F. Hegel, *System of Ethical Life and First Philosophy of Spirit*, translated by H. S. Harris and T. M. Knox (Albany: SUNY Press, 1979). For a similar assessment of Hegel's *System of Ethical Life*, see Axel Honneth, *The Struggle for Recognition.*

14. Quoted in Robert R. Williams, *Recognition,* 85.

15. Williams, *Recognition,* 85.

16. Here Taylor makes an important amendment to Hegel's conception of the family as an idyllic heterosexual domain of unmediated recognition. The amendment is that Taylor does not assume, as does Hegel, that the home is nonconflictual. As feminist critics have correctly pointed out, Hegel completely discounts the fact that the home too has to be a site of struggle, that the bourgeois triangle of mother-father-child is by no means an ideal model. For Hegel's own description, see his *System of Ethical Life*. For a feminist critique, see Patricia Jagentowicz Mills, "Hegel and 'The Woman Question': Recognition and Intersubjectivity," in *The Sexism of Social and Political Theory: Women and Reproduction from Plato to Nietzsche*, edited by Lorrenne M. G. Clark and Lynda Lange (Toronto: University of Toronto Press, 1979).

17. Charles Taylor, "The Politics of Recognition," in *Multiculturalism: Examining the Politics of Recognition*, edited by Amy Gutman (Princeton, N.J.: Princeton University Press, 1994), 37.

18. Taylor, "Politics of Recognition," 60.

19. G. W. F. Hegel, *Phenomenology of Spirit* (New York: Oxford University Press, 1977), 111.

20. Hegel, *Phenomenology*, 111.

21. From the fourth section of Hegel's *Phenomenology of Spirit*, as translated by Williams in *Recognition*, 154.

22. Buber does discuss Hegel, for example, in *Between Man and Man*. There, he does not show a debt to Hegel as much as he distances himself from the later Hegel. Martin Buber, *Between Man and Man* (New York: Collier Books, 1965), 137 ff.

23. Martin Buber, *The Knowledge of Man* (London: George Allen & Unwin, 1965), 67.

24. This way of articulating confirmation as "letting the other happen to me" I have gleaned from conversations with John Stewart.

25. Buber, *Between Man and Man*, 114.

26. Hegel, *Phenomenology*, section 4.

27. From the fourth section of Hegel's *Phenomenology of Spirit*, as translated by Williams in *Recognition*, 154.

28. Williams, *Recognition*, 175.

29. Judith Butler, *Gender Trouble* (New York: Routledge, 1990), 138.

30. From Hegel's *Phenomenology*, section 4, as translated in Williams, *Recognition*, 156.

31. Hegel, *Phenomenology*, 156.

32. Jessica Benjamin, *The Bonds of Love* (New York: Pantheon, 1988), 47.

2

Encounters in the Public Sphere: Mirroring

> The class before him is like a mirror of mankind.
> —Martin Buber[1]

> Who does *dat* make me in this public place?
> —Olivia, interpreted

While the distinction between public and private matters is a typical attribute of liberal thought, this distinction is not often couched in terms of interpersonal recognition.[2] When the school has been considered in its public role, little attention has been given to school as a recognitive public space. In this chapter, I will look into the recognitive implications of school as a public space. Using the work of Charles Taylor as a point of departure, I will look at the personal, historical, and political implications of recognition as a public project. While Taylor's work shows the gains of self that are to be achieved by means of public recognition, his work is limited when it comes to thinking about the more uncertain future of recognition in a racist world like our own. Thus, this chapter will also underscore the ambivalent psychological experience of racist recognition and the prospects of using recognitive politics to generate societal (and educational) change. Before fleshing out public recognition, though, I will review various educational notions of public space.

RECENT CONCEPTIONS OF THE SCHOOL AS A PUBLIC SPACE

Even though the school—as a public space—has often been described as different from home, competing conceptions of the school's public role would have us believe different things. One prevalent view of the public sphere is voiced by Vivian Paley. Describing the public nature of school, she writes of the kindergarten class she teaches:

> The children I teach are just emerging from life's deep wells of private perspective: babyhood and family. Possessiveness and jealousy are inescapable concomitants of both conditions. Then, along comes school. It is the first real exposure to the public arena. Children are required to share materials and teachers in a space that belongs to everyone. Within this public space a new concept of open access can develop if we choose to make this a goal.[3]

Paley's words speak to the distinction between public and private. School encounters require a public give-and-take that is different from the give-and-take that goes on in the privacy of one's home. In the public space of the school, one does not have as much in common with classmates and teachers as one has with parents, siblings, relatives, and loved ones.

For Paley, school is a place where private possessiveness needs to be tempered with public sharing. For example, a child must learn that he or she is not the only one who wants to play a certain classroom game; others may want to play too. This may pose problems if the game is set for a limited number of players, or if one child doesn't like to play with certain others. The public space of school may require more sharing and more turn-taking than is required in the privacy of one's home. At school, there are more people vying for scarce resources. Even if resources are available to all, one may not feel comfortable sharing if one doesn't like the person who is asking to share. Paley indicates the psychological difficulties of entering the public arena of school. The student must learn to be less possessive, less jealous, and more sociable with unknown others.

Another understanding of school, one articulated by Maxine Greene, poses the public arena of school in terms of the unique multivoiced communication that is fostered therein among diverse people. Describing the possibilities of education as a practice of freedom, Greene writes,

> The aim is to find (or create) an authentic public space, that is, one in which diverse human beings can appear before one another as, to quote Hannah Arendt, "the best they know how to be." Such a space requires the provision of opportunities for the articulation of multiple perspectives in multiple idioms, out of which something common can be brought into being.[4]

Following Greene, the school is a place for various types of people to speak their own viewpoints. Schools have the public mission to clear a space that facilitates communication between people whose different per-spectives might not otherwise come into contact. For Greene, the place where such a mélange of voices can be heard is a place where freedom is possible, where people can be drawn out of their own individual ways. When various voices come into contact, a unique public idiom can be formed. In the private sphere, such a liberating idiom is not available be-cause people remain ensconced in their own particular ways of knowing and speaking. For Greene, the value of schooling as public activity is that it fosters unforeseen possibility.

The public nature of education has also been posed in terms of the school's role in a deliberative democratic society. Walter Parker describes school as a place where people can learn how to work together to negoti-ate common goals while still sustaining the identifications that flourish in the private sphere.

> The larger public is, in effect, a normative grid that binds citizens together in a broad association, an essential purpose of which is to protect and even nur-ture individuals and the little publics. Members of a larger public are not praying together or singing the same songs or laughing at the same jokes or growing closer at the telling of the same stories, and it is because of that that the larger public can be portrayed as a thin community rather than a thick one, or a cool association rather than a warm one.[5]

Following this democratic understanding of the public, the school is a common place where people of diverse identities and opinions come to-gether to deliberate, to negotiate, to compromise, or to decide on policies that will foster a common democracy that encourages diverse identities. Public spaces such as schools foster the sorts of deliberative opportunities that are central to making sure a democracy remains pluralistic. Students learn how to be pluralistic and open-minded (qualities essential to demo-cratic citizenship) by means of public discourse.

What is common to these liberal conceptions of school, as they are artic-ulated in the works of Paley, Greene, and Parker, is the assumption that the private self needs to learn a new sociable way of proceeding while sojourning in the public sphere. Paley's work evokes a narrative that pub-lic life ought to overcome the narcissism of private identity. In the work of Greene can be found the following liberal refrain: The chorus of public idiom replaces, at least temporarily, the secluded idioms that obtain in the private sphere. Parker echoes the discourse that the challenge of democratic interaction in a "larger public," such as school, is to deliberate over rules and texts that mediate between various private affiliations. These conceptions of school hold fast to liberal understanding of the ongoing tension between private interest and public community.[6] Whether public space is an arena for overcoming narcissism, a venue for a newly constructed idiom, or a place for negotiation, private identity is seen as giving up a bit of its exclusive particularity in order to become more sociable in the public arena of school.

RECOGNITION AND THE PUBLIC SPACE OF SCHOOL

Charles Taylor, in his work on recognition, offers a very different way of thinking about the public space of school. What most liberal conceptions do not speak to is the possibility that one's particularity, one's very identity, is itself needy, vulnerable, malleable, and even multiple in public spaces such as the school. Taylor's understanding of the public sphere addresses this possibility. Instead of a private self that accedes to public commonalities, Taylor describes a private self that is dramatically affected by public commonalities. A recognitive understanding of the public sphere translates questions of non-narcissism, a common idiom, and democratic interaction into the following sorts of questions: What happens to private identity when one confronts others? How does one's identity change when one joins a common conversation? How does democratic interaction affect private identity? These sorts of questions are raised when the encounter is figured into the equation. Instead of assuming that private identity needs to retreat, be overcome, or be subject to legislation, a recognitive perspective explores how the self changes as a result of the public encounter. Whereas many liberal conceptions assume that the private self is stable enough to move into the public arena, to go about its business of compromise, language-changing, and negotiation, and then move back into the comfortable milieu of private life unaffected, Taylor describes the public self as always affected by the presence of an other. To return to Olivia's term, one's public identity is a matter of who *dat* makes me.

How does Taylor justify his recognitive understanding of public space? Although I sketched out Taylor's recognitive understanding of multiculturalism earlier, I have not yet spoken of the historical logic behind his argument. This is indeed a strength of Taylor's work on recognition. He not only offers a useful description of the public encounter, he also shows the historical logic behind the self's need for recognition. To backtrack a bit and relate Taylor's understanding of the modern self vis-à-vis the premodern self, modern public recognition is the successor to premodern conceptions of "honor." In premodern times, when societies were more stratified, honor was sought in the public sphere but was not equally available to all. Premodern honor was a zero-sum game. As Taylor notes, "for some to have honor in this sense, it is essential that not everyone have it."[7] Individuals gained recognition by means of family bonds and ties with significant others, but in the context of the wider society, there was not a great opportunity for recognitive affirmation or disaffirmation. Except for the possibility of attaining special honorific status, the public self was presaturated with social significance. Most individuals knew their places in society. Public recognition was not available to just anyone because social rank was more fixed. Special distinctions of honor were rarely achieved, and were achieved in any case at the expense of the public distinction of others.

In contrast, Taylor explains that modern societies aspire to equality and egalitarianism. Modern individuals require a form of public recognition that is different from honor. If democratic societies promote equality of rank in the public sphere, then how is one person to be distinguished from another? If each person is not presaturated with social rank, if rank is, at least in theory, discounted, then individuals do not need to know where they stand, because each individual is supposed to be equal. In an egalitarian society, it's not as much *where* one stands as it is *who* one stands. Rank is not as much an issue as cultural identity is. According to Taylor, the modern individual is a dialogic self who turns from herself toward an other for this *who*. I look to someone else to find out who I am—this is where the need for recognition comes in. The modern self does not arrive on the public scene prerecognized. He or she is not presaturated with social significance.

If Taylor is correct, the modern flattening-out of societies puts people in a position to *require* public recognition. Whereas recognitive encounters have long been familiar and ongoing in the intimate sphere, the current configuration of democratic societies maintains a situation where the self needs recognition on the public scene. Thus, Taylor usefully highlights the larger historical and political milieu of self-recognition.

PUBLIC MIRRORING IN SCHOOLS: THE TEXTUAL AND THE INTERPERSONAL ENCOUNTER

With Taylor's historical argument for the importance of public acknowledgment in mind, one way to describe the event of public recognition in schools is to speak in terms of mirrors. That is to say, when I enter the public sphere, I need someone, or some thing, that will mirror back to me an affirming sense of who I am.[8]

Taylor explains societal mirroring as follows:

> our identity is partly shaped by recognition or its absence, often by *misrecognition* of others, and so a person or group of people can suffer real damage, real distortion, if the people or society *mirror back to them* a confining or demeaning or contemptible picture of themselves.[9]

The modern public individual is dependent upon an other for a mirroring of who he or she is. As Taylor points out, such mirroring can sometimes be "demeaning or contemptible." That is to say, the self not only needs mirror recognition in the public sphere, such recognition must not be malrecognition. Public mirroring of self by an other is essential in societies that aim to be egalitarian and fluid.

Following the logic of Taylor's account of recognition, the school is an important venue for mirroring because of its public nature. The self needs acknowledgment in the public place of school. Unlike the home or other spaces in which one seeks recognition from friends or significant others, one must find oneself anew in the public arena of school. When the student enters school, he or she begins to learn how to seek recognition from non–significant others who can mirror back a public version of him or her. Such educational recognition is central to one's sense of self in the public space of a nonhierarchical society.

The mirror metaphor that Taylor uses, and that I am choosing to highlight in order to underscore the public role of recognition, should not simply be construed as signifying that individuals need to "find themselves" in the public encounter, or that individuals need to find an untarnished reflection. Mirrors not only "reflect" us, they constitute us. When we look at a mirror, we not only look to see who we already were, we also gain information about ourselves. The mirrored image gained by looking at the silver glass on a wall, as well as the mirrored image provided by the other with whom we come into contact, are both reflective and constitutive. We run to a mirror not only in order to find out what we already know, but also to gain a sense of self that is new and thus constitutive. Mirrors would be redundant if we already knew what they had in store. This double mode of reflection and constitution during the public encounter is precisely why the recognitive interchange is both promising and uncertain. Mirroring brings on a new sense of self at the same time that it solidifies the old sense. The encounter is reflective and reflexive as it both portrays the self and works on the self.

While the present study employs Taylor's mirror metaphor to think about public recognition, I am critical of his liberal understanding of mirroring because it fails to think about the constitutive side to mirroring in any complex way. Taylor's notion of mirroring assumes that the private and cultural horizons of individuals need to be reflected, but he fails to emphasize that the mirroring process itself is fraught with uncertainty. Thus, by requiring that the cultural horizon of the one-recognizing be something that exists before the mirroring encounter, Taylor fails to complexify the productive workings of recognitive mirroring. Although it might be convenient to think of an individual (and "individual" is precisely the concept that Taylor cannot give up) as possessing some cultural horizon that is either reflected or not during the encounter, mirroring is already at work. The shortcoming of a theory such as Taylor's is that it always starts with the private individual as pregiven, as if the individual completely precedes the mirror experience. This can hardly be the case, since mirrors create as well represent.

With this general understanding of mirror reflection and mirror constitution, I turn to the educational relevance of public mirroring. At least two types of mirroring can come into play within the classroom walls: curricular mirroring and interpersonal mirroring. While curricular mirroring refers to the sorts of reflections the self finds by way of the textual encounter, interpersonal mirroring refers to the fleshly encounter. I can "see" myself on the written page, or I can "see" myself in another's eyes.

Textual Mirroring

I begin with textual encounters. A recognitive understanding of the classroom sheds light on the relevance of who is represented in the curriculum. One way that students can be recognized in the public space of school is by looking to written sources for mirroring. While the private arena is a place where one is generally steeped in one's own familiar cul-

ture, the public space of schools is likely to bring unfamiliarity—a lack of
the familiar recognition from others who share one's own background.
The need for diverse curricular representations across the curriculum can
be construed in terms of the question, Who? Who is getting recognition
through the books that are being read in classrooms? Who is getting recognition through other types of content materials? Whose stories are
being told? Who is being represented and who is being left out? The importance of which particular cultural representations are textually available in schools becomes evident when we consider the shifted cultural
expectations that so many students experience by virtue of entering the
public space of school. One way a student can be recognized in school is
for his or her story to be told. Who hears his or her story in places such
as schools can be crucial to whose dignity is sustained in the larger cultural arena.[10]

Taylor explains the link between school curriculum and public recognition as follows:

> The reason for these proposed changes [in curriculum] is not, or not mainly,
> that all students may be missing something important through the exclusion
> of a certain gender or certain races or cultures, but rather that women and
> students from the excluded groups are given, either directly or by omission,
> a demeaning picture of themselves, as though all creativity and worth is in-
> hered in males of European provenance.[11]

In this passage, Taylor maps his recognitive understanding of self onto
the multiculturalist goal of curriculum integration. He says that the
human need for mirroring is the most pressing reason for advocating a
more broadly representative curriculum. Curriculum needs to be equita-
bly representative so that all students can find positive mirroring therein.

Taylor's claim that recognition is the fundamental reason for curricular
changes is too sweeping. It is misguided in the sense that there may be
other reasons for curricular change that are not at all based on the need
for recognition. For example, a critical exegesis of historical events, such
as one finds in Howard Zinn's *A People's History of the United States*, may
not have been written in order to "reflect" better on a nonhegemonic
group, nor on individual members of that group. The purpose of Zinn's
version of history may rather be to get at some "truths" that have been
heretofore unpublished. Such a text may or may not be intended to afford
individual or group recognition. Or, as an English teacher at a high

school, I may choose Toni Morrison's *Sula* not because I want to include the work of an African American woman novelist on my syllabus, but because I believe it deals with the theme of abjection more powerfully than any other novel.[12]

Moreover, advocates of multicultural education have argued that there are a number of reasons why the curriculum should be diversified. James Banks notes that curriculum should be more culturally representative for a number of reasons: to empower students of color politically; to reduce racial prejudices; to create a more equitable school environment; to increase academic achievement of students from different ethnic, cultural, and gender groups; and to enable students to look from different perspectives with increasing facility.[13]

Taylor's insight is an important one, however, even if recognition is not the sole reason for infusing curriculum with diverse cultural stories. The modern need for public recognition is a significant way to think through whether educators take the time and effort to ensure that students see themselves mirrored in texts. A liberal understanding of recognition yields this important contribution to multicultural theory: Curriculum changes are necessary because students need textual mirroring in the public space of the school. On one hand, multicultural efforts to transform the curriculum by advocating that all cultural groups be reflected in curricula implicitly acknowledge the benefit one derives from being mirrored in texts. On the other hand, the liberal understanding of recognition puts such mirroring in spatial, historical, and interpersonal context.[14]

Positive textual images are recognitively significant in public spaces such as schools during modern egalitarian times, and given the needy nature of personhood. A diverse curriculum is necessary because the selves of students are implicated in what they read and learn. To put this another way, if the self is "constituted in conversation," as Taylor says, then textual representation must be seen as part of "the conversation that we ourselves are," to use Hans-Georg Gadamer's phrase.[15] As atomistic, disconnected selves, students would not benefit from the mirror aspect of curricular changes. But, if the modern self exists in relation to other people and to what gets said and written by other people, then it is crucial to emphasize the significance of textual mirroring.

Public Mirroring and the Multiculturalism Debate

Taylor's mirror conception of curricular representation is particularly helpful, as it teases out some of the unspoken assumptions within current debates over multiculturalism. Taylor's discourse on the self-in-search-of-mirroring is useful for thinking through the positions of those who assail, as well as those who advocate, curricular change. Following Taylor, public recognition is certainly one reason to advocate a multicultural curriculum. Accentuating this one reason clarifies some nuances of the debate over multiculturalism.

Taylor's mirror model of recognition is helpful because it offers an optic lens through which to scrutinize the recommendations of anti-multiculturalists, such as E. D. Hirsch, who advocate a "core curriculum." Taylor's discussion of mirror recognition helps to highlight some of Hirsch's assumptions about the atomistic nature of self.

In *The Schools We Need and Why We Don't Have Them*, Hirsch takes odds with progressive education in general and multiculturalism in particular.[16] He defends a national core curriculum that would not mirror the cultural identities of many of today's students. By a "core curriculum," Hirsch means a common set of learning for each child in America. Such a curriculum, Hirsch maintains, would enhance the academic achievement of students whom Hirsch calls "disadvantaged." He claims that the lack of a core curriculum in America has left us in a state of "academic incoherence" that precludes effective pedagogy. The lack of a core curriculum, following Hirsch, keeps us from having "the schools we need."

Even if we look past the condescending rhetoric of an educator who conflates myriad cultural and economic circumstances into one lump descriptor of "disadvantaged students," we can still ask what ontological assumptions and what considerations of self undergird the concept of a core curriculum. Taylor's notion of public recognition helps to clarify the failure of Hirsch to "recognize" recognition. Simply put, a core curriculum does not aspire to promote mirror recognition.[17] Such a curriculum assumes that one does not need to find one's self at school. Whether a student finds positive mirroring at school is not as important as that he or she be "filled" with a core set of learnings. The logic behind a core curriculum is that students leave their need for recognition outside the school door. As Hirsch explains, "It is a fundamental injustice that what American children are enabled to learn in school should be determined by what their homes have already given them."[18] Hirsch implicitly argues that students are not needful of recognition in the public space of school. The school is not a place where student identities need to be mirrored. The student self is spectatorial, detached, and atomistic.

Hirsch's depository metaphors back up this atomistic version of students. Using the rhetoric of "intellectual capital," Hirsch implicitly embraces an instrumental version of self that precludes a substantive discussion of the recognitive elements of curriculum. The self is rhetorically situated as a bank to be filled with capital.[19] Schooling is all about what can be done by a stable self with the information given at school. There is no possibility that identity can actually be at stake in the school. "Intellectual capital" is either useful or not useful, but it has no impact on the self. To return to Olivia's question, there is no room for the question "Who does dat make me?"

Taylor's notion of public mirroring further underscores how Hirsch conveniently conflates the cognitive acquisition of information with cultural recognition.[20] This conflation is evident in Hirsch's statement that students' educational experiences should not be "determined by what their homes have already given them." The reader of *The Schools We Need* is left with the impression that one's cultural horizon amounts to no more than the grade it lets one get on a classroom test. Hirsch downgrades cultural identity to the status of facts like "the square root of 49 is 7."

Hirsch's view of the student self is nothing to argue with per se. If he decides that selves are atomistic, that is his own business, his own worldview. However, upon scrutiny, Hirsch does not advocate an atomistic view of the self for all students as much as he advocates it for those students who do not find themselves reflected in the core curriculum. The unspoken entailments of a core curriculum subscribe to a duplicitous view of student selves. For students who do not find themselves mirrored in the curriculum, Hirsch does not deem that recognition essential. Mirror recognition is foreclosed in such cases.

Some students will find themselves mirrored in the core curriculum. For these students, there is a sort of ontological double standard. While Hirsch explicitly rejects the need for mirror recognition for some students, he conveniently leaves open the possibility for other students to benefit from such recognition. For example, he has no problem with students' education being "determined by what their homes have already given them" if those students are a part of the hegemonic culture. For Hirsch, mirror recognition is not essential, so some students might as well go without. That other students are granted curricular recognition, and that there is a discrepancy between some students and others with regard to mirror recognition, is not Hirsch's concern.

In addition to noting the ontological double standard of the core curriculum, it is important to note the political territory that such a curriculum keeps cultural groups from occupying. As Taylor argues, curricular representation is not only about personal recognition, it is also a matter of cultural groups who find in texts a reason and a cause for organization. He explains that "the struggle for freedom and equality must therefore pass through a revision of these [textual] images."[21] Texts and symbolic representations are bases for political configurations. To say that curriculum should not be contested, that it should be uniform across the country, is to deprive underrepresented groups of an important locus for political struggle. Texts are important not only for the self-recognition of individuals but for the recognition of entire groups.[22] A recognitive understanding of social action suggests that selves change and that groups should stake out political positions as a result of the mirroring that is or is not provided in public places like schools. Students and social groups are not repositories, but people continually in the making.

Interpersonal Mirroring

In this section, I move from textual to interpersonal mirroring. I will focus on a literary account of interpersonal mirroring found in James Weldon Johnson's *The Autobiography of an Ex-Colored Man*. Johnson presents a classroom experience that is both literally and metaphorically an instance of mirror recognition in the public arena.[23] As I will show, Johnson's narrative both exemplifies and challenges Taylor's model of public recognition.

The narrator tells the following story about his experiences as a light-skinned African American student in a racially mixed elementary school. He has just moved from Georgia to Connecticut.[24] He is nine years old, and this is the first time that he has attended school. From the very beginning, he excels in his courses. He is a piano prodigy and one of the quicker students in his class.

As time passes, the protagonist becomes entangled in the web of racism spun among the students in his class. He is snared on the white side of a racist dichotomy that pits white children against black children. Racism, in their classroom, causes white students to wield insults and hurl objects at their black classmates.

At nine years old, he has always identified himself as white. His white identity relies not so much on his own whiteness per se, but more on the difference between himself and other students who are not white. He learns to side with the white children at crucial moments, particularly when they band together to harass black students. One such student is named "Shiny."

As the protagonist explains, he actually likes Shiny most of the time, yet it does not take him long to discover that even though Shiny is the most intelligent boy in class, he is still supposed to look down on Shiny because Shiny is black. He is supposed to look down on all of the black boys and girls. Sometimes he and other white students walk behind the black boys and girls on their way home, and they shout at them: "Nigger, nigger, never die, / Black face and shiny eye."[25] On one such afternoon, one of the black boys turns on the protagonist's group of white friends and throws a slate at them. One of the white boys is struck by the slate, and it gashes his lip. The protagonist and his companions run after the boy who has thrown the slate. The group of white children pelts all of the black children until they disperse in several directions.

In this, his first year of school, the protagonist acts as racist, as epithet thrower, and as stone thrower. At this point in his life, he considers himself white and superior. The students around him seem to agree. He does not yet know that he himself will soon be on the other side of this vicious exchange. He himself will soon be identified as black. His teacher will point this fact out to him. She will point it out to all of the students in his class. She will act as a mirror who will reflect him in a different hue.

One day the principal comes into his classroom. For some reason, the principal asks all of the white students to stand for a moment.[26] The protagonist rises with the other white children. The teacher looks at him and says, "You sit down for the present." He is shocked. He falls into a kind of stupor until school is dismissed. After school is out, a few of the white boys begin to jeer at him. He is now on the other side of a racial divide. "Oh, you're a nigger too," they say. And he hears some of the black children say, "We knew he was colored."[27]

The teacher reflects the protagonist back to himself in a way that the rest of his childhood as a white boy has not prepared him for. She acts as a mirror that informs him how he will "look" to others henceforth. He feels the teacher's words were necessary, yet he cannot escape the personal pain he feels as a result. As he puts it, "Perhaps it had to be done, but I have never forgiven the woman who did it so cruelly."[28]

As if to parallel the mirroring effect of his teacher's words, he goes straight home and stares into his own looking glass. At first he is afraid to look, but then he stares into the mirror long and earnestly. In the look-

ing glass he still sees a white face, in spite of what his teacher and classmates have told him. As the narrator describes it,

> I was accustomed to hear remarks about my beauty; but now, for the first
> time, I became conscious of it and recognized it. I noticed the ivory whiteness
> of my skin, the beauty of my mouth, the size and liquid darkness of my
> eyes.[29]

After looking in the mirror, he asks his mother if he is white or not. She
tells him that he is not white. He asks her, "Am I a nigger?" She replies,
"No, my darling, you are not a nigger . . . if anyone calls you a nigger,
don't notice them."[30]

Both in story and in the symbolism of the looking glass, Johnson emphasizes the role that this teacher has in reflecting who the narrator will
be both to himself and to others. Looked at with Taylor's notion of public
recognition in mind, the protagonist's experience in his first year of
school marks a transition from the private to the public sphere. It is a transition from mirror recognition by significant others to mirror recognition
by members of society at large. At home, the protagonist has learned that
he is white. In the private sphere, his racial recognition as white has not
been particularly problematic. Following the liberal account of recognition, we might assume that he had other struggles for recognition at
home, struggles to gain the recognition of "significant others." Indeed,
the first nine years of his life are marked, as are the lives of most children,
by the need for recognition from parents and elders, but race has not been
an explicit issue at home. He has needed recognition as a child, as a piano
player, as a son, but he has not been preoccupied with gaining recognition as a member of a particular race.[31] Reminiscent of the love-bound,
private recognition that Hegel describes as "recognition without conflict
of will," racial recognition has been unproblematic in the private sphere
of this student's life.[32]

Then the student arrives at the public venue of school. At this point, he
finds that he must deal with another sort of recognition—racial recognition. At school he experiences the sort of public mirroring that Taylor articulates. The self of recognition in the public sphere is most often a cultural self, a gendered self, a raced self, or a self of ethnicity. In other
words, the sorts of recognitive interactions that confirm a sense of dignity
on the one-recognized are most likely to be identity horizons that are held
by that individual to be salient. But because individuals are, in Taylor's

view, grounded in community life, such ascriptions are likely to be identity horizons that are shared with others. Cultured, gendered, racial, and ethnic identities are prime examples. Mapping Taylor's understanding onto Johnson's text, we see that a student's recognitive experience consists of being recognized against the backdrop of his or her cultural horizon, and such recognition comes in the form of mirroring by an other. In this student's case, the other who acts as mirror is his teacher. She mirrors his African American identity to him in what he identifies as a shocking epiphany: "It may be that she will never know that she gave me a sword-thrust that day in school which was years in healing."[33]

This student's experience of mirroring in the public sphere is one of misrecognition because black identity has been subject to ridicule in this classroom. It is, in Taylor's words, an instance in which a person or group of people suffers "real damage, real distortion, if the people or society around them mirror back to them a confining or demeaning or contemptible picture of themselves."[34] The quality of this public recognition is altogether different from the mirroring this student gets in the private sphere, and from what he had previously received in the public space of school.

Psychic Aspects of the Encounter

While Taylor's notion of public recognition does help to unpack Johnson's narrative, *The Autobiography* speaks to psychological nuances of public/ private recognition that are not available in Taylor's account. Liberal recognition, as we have discussed it so far, primarily has to do with conscious thought. Hegel, upon whom Taylor draws heavily, describes the consciousness of the struggle for recognition in the following terms: "Self-consciousness exists in and for itself when, and by the fact that, it so exists for another; that is, it exists only in being acknowledged."[35] Hegelian mirroring enables one to be conscious of who one is. Mirror recognition by an other gives me an image of what it means to be me. In Olivia's words, this version of mirror recognition happens when *dat* person lets me know who I am. This sort of recognition depends upon what I can know consciously. Even the word *recognition*, etymologically linked as it is to rethinking, to re-cognition, implies a certain conscious rumination. In the presence of an other, one rethinks who one is. Our discussion of recognition has so far been couched in terms of conscious discovery.

Johnson theorizes a psychic side to recognition. In Johnson's narrative, mirror recognition seems more complicated than the trope of conscious discovery suggests. Johnson's student does not simply change his conscious thinking when he discovers that he is black. There are tensions and ambivalences in his mirror experience. There are tensions between past understandings of self and present revelations, between harbored prejudices and newfound identity, between who one was and who one will be. There are ambivalences concerning how he will recognize himself from now on. Will he recognize himself through the mirror image that his teacher and classmates have offered him, or will he recognize himself as he always has, as in the mirror in his hallway at home? These tensions and ambivalences suggest that recognition is not as simple as coming to consciousness anew. They suggest that disparate understandings of self may intersect in a space that is not as logical as conscious thought, that the illogic of mirror recognition may inhabit a space that is not available to conscious rethinking.

Johnson points out that the public/private split is not psychically clean. For example, when the student goes home to examine himself in the looking glass, he sees that he looks white, yet he knows that he has been labeled black in the public space of the classroom. There is now a disjuncture of identity between what he knows of himself at home and what he knows of himself at school. It is not just that his racial identity has been disparaged at school. Rather, a fundamental fragmenting of identity takes place as a result of public recognition. For this student, identity is constituted differently at school than it is at home. Looking in the mirror, the self holds two incommensurate identities at once in what Freud has described as an "uncanny" experience.[36] It is an experience of *"das Unheimlich,"* an experience that is, following the German etymology, homely and familiar but at the same time foreign and unknown; it is an experience that bears allegiance to both its private (homely) identity and public (unknown) identity. The student in Johnson's narrative is both white and black, both affirmed and rejected. There is now an incongruence of identity that lingers in the psyche.

If one psychic ambivalence consists of the bifurcated nature of the student's public/private identity, another is to be found completely within his public experience, lodged in the intersection of black identity and racist discourse. There are two parts to this student's experience of recognition: the first is the discovery that he is black, and the second is the concomitant realization that being black positions him on the receiving end of racist speech and acts. The racist web of the classroom leaves Johnson's student straddled between finding out that he is black and finding out that he will therefore be subject to racist acts in the future. This recognitive ambivalence is echoed in the different ways that his classmates respond to the recognition scene. The white children say, "Oh, you're a nigger too," while the black children remark to each other that "we knew he was colored."[37] These two comments highlight the psychic ambivalence that is at play between racist positioning and racial identity in the public space of school.

Franz Fanon has explored this psychic ambivalence of public recognition in *Black Skins, White Masks*. He describes his "fragmenting" mirror experience as a black man on the streets of France. While still living in his homeland of Antilles, Fanon had not felt his own racial identity to be stigmatizing or even salient. Upon being accosted in the street by white people in France, he realizes for the first time that his blackness is a salient aspect of his identity. This racial mirroring derives from the fact that Fanon is now in a culture that reflects his blackness in a negative light. Fanon describes his experience like this:

> [Someone shouted] "Dirty nigger!" Or simply, "Look, a Negro!"
> I came into the world imbued with the will to find a meaning in things, my spirit filled with the desire to attain to the source of the world, and then I found that I was an object in the midst of other objects.
> Sealed into that crushing objecthood, I turned beseechingly to others. . . .
> I was indignant; I demanded an explanation. Nothing happened. I *burst apart*. Now the fragments have been put together again by *another self*.[38]

In this account, Fanon emphasizes the alienating effects of recognition in societies that are steeped in racism. In a society where racist discourse abounds, it doesn't matter if one is recognized by means of "a confining or demeaning or contemptible picture" or not.[39] It doesn't matter if one hears the slur "dirty nigger," or simply "Look, a Negro." Whatever the case, being identified as a black person in a racist society leads to alienation.

The psyche has the ability to maintain a double register in which there may be an incongruence between how one is recognized in public and how one is recognized in private. The mirror experience may create this ambivalence when a person is constructed as "other" in the public sphere. Fanon describes this forced psychic ambivalence of an "other" who experiences public recognition when he notes that "not only must the black man be black; he must be black in relation to the white man."[40]

Racist discourse carries with it a psychically alienating component whether that discourse goes unsaid or said. This psychic description of racist recognition challenges the simplicity of Taylor's liberal description of recognition. Ignoring the psychosocial nexus of mirror recognition, Taylor implies that positive recognition can be a matter of voluntary image-making on the part of the one-who-mirrors. He implies that it is mostly up to the will of the one-who-mirrors to mirror in a way that is not "confining or demeaning or contemptible." He does not sufficiently delve into the psychic implications of mirroring that are often deeply embedded in historical and economic circumstances, circumstances that may unconsciously overshadow the ameliorative potential of a given representation. As Johnson and Fanon describe it, the psyche is savvy enough to hold on to multiple versions of identity at once. The psyche will not give up prevalent notions of cultural identity at the sight of a mirror. The constitutive quality of mirroring depends both on the meaning of the "picture" that is offered of the self and on what that picture signifies in the broader culture.

Mapping the private/public split directly onto psychic life, the cultural mirroring one receives in public spaces such as schools is a "secondary mirror stage."[41] Here I am using Jacques Lacan's understanding of the primary mirror stage that infants go through during their second year of life.[42] According to Lacan, one's sense of self is first established in front of a mirror at this early age. This primary mirror stage is a formative moment in the development of the self insofar as one learns to look elsewhere to see who one is. The secondary mirror stage is likewise formative. In the public arena, one learns to look to unknown others in order to shore up a mirror image of self.

Fanon's work draws on Lacanian psychoanalysis, and Fanon's description of the self-fragmentation ("I burst apart") occurring in racist societies is a reminder that psychic mirroring has a cultural as well as a private dimension. Although the child's primary mirror experience may not derive from cultural aspects of difference when it takes place in private surroundings, there is bound to be a secondary mirror stage that is heavily influenced by the cultural reflection that one receives in public. Cultural and private images of self may not only match up, be absent, or be demeaning, they may also coexist in the psyche. A psychic understanding of secondary mirroring speaks to how identity positions become multiple and negotiated as a person's cultural identity becomes public.

But if one insight offered by both Johnson and Fanon is that the self negotiates multiple identity positions because of the secondary mirror stage, the more central part of their project is to show how the secondary mirror stage, while being psychological, is heavily mediated by social expectations and by social oppressions. The secondary mirror stage can be mediated by social circumstances that need to be improved. In concert with this social message, the next section will examine how the public experience of mirroring can be used as a key for social change.

BRIDGING PERSONAL AND SOCIAL RECOGNITION

So far, we have considered public recognition mainly on a personal or psychological level, but personal recognition in the public sphere can also be used as a linchpin for social action. Personal recognition and social action are undeniably linked: if one person encounters misrecognition because of his or her cultural, ethnic, race, gender, sexual, or class affiliation, it is likely that there are discourses at work in the culture at large whereby others may similarly encounter misrecognition. For example, if I suffer misrecognition of my sexual identity, it is likely that others of my persuasion will similarly suffer. On the basis of this logic, it makes sense to use a personal affront to one's dignity—a personal instance of misrecognition—as a rallying point for larger social action. Personal misrecognition can be taken as a cue for a larger social need.

Axel Honneth has done extensive work on the implications of interpersonal recognition for a broad program of social justice. He describes this link as "an asserted connection between moral disrespect and social struggle."[43] The personal experience of misrecognition is an important connection precisely because "formal" rallying points for social action are sometimes made mysteriously unavailable in a democratic state such as ours. When economic disadvantage is glossed over as personal lack of ambition; when governmental underrepresentation is construed as constituency apathy at the polls; when institutional exclusion is couched in terms of educational "best practices" like tracking, or in terms of a lack of individual effort; and when systemic exclusion of groups is written off as personal failure, then cultural groups need a rallying point around which to organize. Honneth emphasizes the importance of personal feelings as a gauge by which to measure whether social conditions need to be improved. Such feeling may or may not coincide with economic opportunity, with political representation, or with institutional exclusion. That is, one may feel misrecognized without being "officially" economically disadvantaged, without being "officially" underrepresented in government, without being "formally" barred from services in institutions such as schools. The rallying point of personal misrecognition does not rely on any one single factor, such as having money, being able to vote candidates into office, or having access to education.

Honneth explains the difference between group action that is goods-based and action that is recognition-based as follows:

> In the first case [in a goods-based model], we are dealing with the analysis of competition for scarce goods, whereas in the second case, we are dealing with the analysis of a struggle over the intersubjective conditions for personal integrity.[44]

The assumption of a social project based on recognition is that personal feelings count enough to take a political stand.[45]

This link between the recognition and social action is what Honneth calls a "semantic bridge" for a politics of recognition.

> There must be a semantic bridge between impersonal aspirations of a social movement and their participants' private experiences of injury, a bridge that is sturdy enough to enable the development of collective identity.[46]

Honneth argues that at present there is not such a semantic bridge available for social action. There is no clear way to articulate the relationship between personal affronts to dignity and the larger social implications that such affronts may signify. A semantic bridge of recognition can give voice to that relationship. I suggest that such semantics should consist of at least three components.

Misrecognition

First, when one person suffers *misrecognition* in the public sphere, whether it be the result of what Taylor calls a "confining or demeaning or diminished" mirroring, or because of hate speech, or because of a result of personal ill-treatment, or because one simply does not feel "there" in a certain public space, then there is reason to assume that there are, in general, such misrecognitive discourses that are available in general for public use. That is, if it is easy for one person to ill treat another, it is likely that there is already a lexicon of ill treatment available. There is already misrecognition "in the air." A language of recognition enables one to call attention to the larger societal modes of misrecognition that are at work.

Articulation

Second, the act of moral affront must be *articulated* by those who experience misrecognition. One cannot decide from above whether a person experiences recognition or misrecognition. When recognition is used as a measure for social action, there will be "insider" and "outsider" perspectives.[47] An "insider" will have a quality of insight into his or her experience of recognition that an "outsider" will not be privy to. In general, others must accept that my experience of recognition or misrecognition is best voiced by me.

Social Action

Third, it is essential to base broad *social action* on behalf of others who have experienced misrecognition. When one person, or a group of people, feels misrecognized in the public sphere, then it is justifiable for others to take up the cause of that person or those people. Taking up the cause of another should be done not only to improve that isolated instance but with the hope that such an improvement can be a cue for broader social change. An affront to dignity needs to be taken up by more than just those who experienced the affront. Allies need to get on board. Because an affront to one person's dignity is likely to be symptomatic of a more systemic or discursively entrenched set of practices, group action is necessary on behalf of the misrecognition of one, or a few, individuals.

Disturbingly, a struggle against misrecognition must be fraught with threat as well as aspiration. If there be recognition in the first place, there will be the threat and perhaps the inevitability of misrecognition at the same time. To be recognized, whether one has sought that recognition or is a passive recipient of it, first of all entails a certain submission to the other who is doing the recognizing. It entails that there be teacher or a friend, for example, who is in the position of granting or withholding recognition. Even if the mirror is ameliorative, the one recognized is never in full control of when that recognition takes place or whether even that positive recognition will catch in a way that secures long-standing dignity. To struggle against recognition is at the same time to risk being misrecognized by mirrors that are out of one's control. The first threat is of course that one will be malrecognized by virtue of a "demeaning or contemptible" picture. More than that, there is the practice of depending upon an other that is dangerous insofar as the other is by definition not me and not in my control.

The value of Taylor's historical understanding of recognition is that it underscores a historical scenario that may well be necessary in societies that strive for egalitarianism—a scenario of recognitive encounters in the public sphere. The irony of Taylor's description is that the very act of seeking recognition from significant others, or even depending passively on others for that recognition, may be an act of submission to those who are recognizing, thus creating a set of unequal relations that undercut the initial gesture toward egalitarianism. Just as I have pointed out earlier with regard to the political project of recognition, the very worst response to such a situation of unequal status between those recognizing and those recognized is for the one-recognized to go it alone. If there is reason to be mindful of recognitive encounters, there is also reason to go at the encounter in solidarity so that even the very act of positive recognition does not become an act of subordination. That recognition is fraught with power relations between self and other is something that Taylor fails to consider fully. To answer such a failing, it is imperative to recall that solidarity is not only something that needs to be reflected qua identity "horizon"; it is also something that needs to be created in order to deal with the threat and the aspiration of recognition.

I have introduced these three components that bridge personal recognition and social action for a specific purpose. Misrecognition is not a personal issue. Especially within schools that tend to reproduce the hierarchies of the larger society, it is most likely that personal affronts to dignity have a larger social meaning. If this is so, and if there is agreement that misrecognition needs to be combated, then it is the obligation of educators and students to look into the links between *personal* misrecognition and *systemic* misrecognition in order to try to combat the latter as well as the former. I see the school not only as a place where this semantic bridge can be established but also as a place where students and teachers can learn to get into the habit of doing so. The school is not only a place where personal and social misrecognition can be combated, it is also a place where students and teachers can learn how to combat misrecognition outside of the classroom doors.

In this chapter, I have looked at the conscious, unconscious, and social considerations of the public encounter with the other. A premise of my analysis has been that the public self is knowable enough to be mirrored, either textually or interpersonally. Is there a model of the encounter with the other that might speak to instances when the other is not so knowable? The next chapter will address this issue of unknowability.

NOTES

1. Martin Buber, *Between Man and Man* (New York: Collier Books), 112.

2. By "public," I do not necessarily refer to the fact that a given school is supported by public money, but instead to the notion that the school needs to carry out the public work of educating students to live in a democracy. There is widespread haziness about how public money actually contributes in any way to the democratic role of schools. These two senses of "public"—the money sense and the civic sense—are often conflated in much the same way that United States foreign policy often conflates capitalism with democracy. I am not saying that public control over school funds does not supply a modicum of contractual limitations to the extension of schools into parochial arenas. Public funds have done little to ensure that schools teach democracy (in the civic sense) that is much deeper than the saying of the Pledge of Allegiance and the observance of important national holidays such as Martin Luther King Jr. Day. For seminal work on the private/public link with regard to schools, see Jane Roland Martin, *The Schoolhome: Rethinking Schools for Changing Families* (Cambridge: Harvard University Press, 1985).

3. Vivian Gussin Paley, *You Can't Say You Can't Play* (Cambridge: Harvard University Press, 1992), 21.

4. Maxine Greene, *The Dialectic of Freedom* (New York: Teachers College Press, 1988), xi.

5. Walter C. Parker, "Navigating the Unity/Diversity Tension in Education for Democracy," *The Social Studies* 88 (1997): 14. See also Parker, "Democracy and Difference," *Theory and Research in Social Education* 25, no. 2 (1997): 220–234.

6. I am not trying to speak here for the entire opus of each of these three authors. For example, it might be argued here that in some of Paley's work, in *The Boy Who Would Be a Helicopter* (Cambridge: Harvard University Press, 1990) for example, she does in fact consider how one's identity changes when one joins a common conversation. Be that as it may, here I am only identifying some commonly articulated liberal discourses—the discourses of nonnarcissism, a common idiom, and democratic interaction—that are indeed reiterated by these three authors in the particular texts I have looked into. The authors may say otherwise elsewhere, but in these particular texts they have invoked some common liberal refrains.

7. Charles Taylor, "The Politics of Recognition," in *Multiculturalism: Examining the Politics of Recognition*, edited by Amy Gutman (Princeton, N.J.: Princeton University Press, 1994), 27.

8. A word about mirrors. In the analysis that follows, I will be using the concept of the mirror both literally and metaphorically. The mirror's literal sense obviously refers to the object that hangs on a wall. Yet the mirror's literal sense is quickly undermined by both the grammatical flexibility of the word "mirror," and by the rich literary uses of the mirror-as-metaphor. The *Oxford English Dictionary* tells us that the word "mirror" is both a noun and a verb. "Mirror" is not only the object on the wall, but also "to reflect or represent something." *The Compact Edition of the Oxford English Dictionary* (Oxford: Oxford University Press, 1971), 1807. The verbal sense of "mirror" widens the notion of the looking glass, advancing the more general connotation of "mirror" as a process by which the image of an object, or in the case of this study the self, is offered to view.

Literary uses of the mirror have long emphasized the metaphorical import of mirroring. One need only think of Narcissus, Lady Macbeth, Alice, or John Ashbery's *Self-Portrait in a Convex Mirror* (New York: Penguin, 1976). In her study of the literary conceptions of mirroring, Jenijoy La Belle describes the "intricate and complex role a mirror plays in the process of recognition, identity, and self-consciousness." Jenijoy La Belle, *Herself Beheld: The Literature of the Looking Glass* (Ithaca, N.Y.: Cornell University Press, 1988), 15. This is all by way of saying that the concept of mirroring is not merely a rhetorical way of describing the liberal conception of recognition. Mirroring is a thick concept whose metaphorical resonance will also invite literary representations into the present study.

9. Taylor, "The Politics of Recognition," 25, emphasis mine.

10. For an investigation into the importance of students' stories being told in the classroom, see Jaylynne N. Hutchinson, *Students on the Margins: Education, Dignity, Stories* (Albany: SUNY Press, 1999).

11. Taylor, "The Politics of Recognition," 65.

12. Howard Zinn, *A People's History of the United States* (New York: Harper Perennial, 1995); Toni Morrison, *Sula* (New York: Knopf, 1974).

13. James Banks, *An Introduction to Multicultural Education* (Boston: Allyn and Bacon, 1994), 11.

14. As Banks puts it, "school knowledge should *reflect* the experiences of all of the nation's citizens" (italics mine). Banks, *An Introduction to Multicultural Education*, 24.

15. Charles Taylor, "The Dialogical Self," in *The Interpretive Turn: Philosphy, Science, Culture*, edited by David Hiley, James Bohman, and Richard Shusterman (Ithaca, N.Y.: Cornell University Press), 314; Hans-Georg Gadamer, *Truth and Method* (New York: Continuum, 1994), 378.

16. E. D. Hirsch, *The Schools We Need and Why We Don't Have Them* (New York: Doubleday, 1996).

17. Except for the few students who already "find themselves" in the curriculum, which I discuss shortly.

18. Hirsch, *The Schools We Need*, 47.

19. For a critique of "banking" models, see Paulo Freire, *Pedagogy of the Oppressed* (New York: Continuum, 1970).

20. I take up this theme of conflating recognition and acquisition of knowledge again in chapter 6.

21. Taylor, "The Politics of Recognition," 66.

22. For commentaries on Hegel's ethical account of recognition and its meaning for politics, see Axel Honneth, *The Struggle for Recognition*, 3–63; and Robert R. Williams, *Hegel's Ethics of Recognition*, wherein Williams argues that intersubjectivity guides *all* of Hegel's ethics and not just the early Jena period writings as is typically assumed.

23. James Weldon Johnson, *The Autobiography of an Ex-Colored Man* (New York: Penguin, 1990). Recently, speaking as a respondent during a symposium on Nietzsche at the Philosophy of Education Society conference (March 26, 1999), Maxine Greene argued that it was important to note the difference between a work of philosophy such as Nietzsche's *Genealogy of Morals* and a work of art such as Thomas Mann's *Death in Venice*. In this work I make no such distinction. If Johnson's text offers a valid theoretical perspective, if it adds to our toolkit for thinking about the encounter, then it is just as valid as a text that claims philosophical authority. The main distinction that I see between a philosophical text and a literary one is in the claims to agency that one *can* attribute to a philosophical text and that one *cannot* attribute to a literary text. I do not assume, for example, that Johnson meant his text to address recognition, and therefore I cannot chastise his theorizing of encounter for its lack of completeness or for its ignorance of certain recognitive aspects. To some extent, a text like Johnson's is preprotected against assault while it remains wholly available for application. One cannot say the same about Taylor's text. Taylor has philosophical agency in the sense that he is speaking directly to recognition. I make this point about philosophy vis-à-vis literature in order to set the stage for how I will be employing literary texts in this work.

24. I call the narrator "he" in my own presentation because there is no textual acknowledgment of his actual name. This unnamed status is itself a historical and textual marker of the material conditions of production that surrounded being an African American author in America in the early twentieth century. *The Autobiography* is not an actual autobiography but is a piece of fiction that was titled as such because African American writing at the time appealed best to white audiences when it followed the generic traits of slave narratives and testifying confessionals. (See William L. Andrews's introduction in *The Autobiography*.) As historical and textual marker, the unnamed status of the narrator is symbolic of the requirement that Johnson could write a selling piece of fiction only under the guise of reality. He had to be both hyperreal and not real at all, both named and unnamed.

25. Johnson, *The Autobiography*, 10.

26. I say "for some reason" here because the reason the principal asks the white students to stand is not clear in the text. Johnson writes, "the principal came into our room and, after talking to the teacher, for some reason said: 'I wish all of the white scholars to stand for a moment.' " As I read this scene, the very ambiguity of this "some reason" is a textual cue to the fundamental illogic of racism. The segregation of the students presents a narrative difficulty that Johnson judiciously leaves in a state of illogic.

27. Johnson, *The Autobiography*, 11.

28. Johnson, *The Autobiography*, 12.

29. Johnson, *The Autobiography*, 11.

30. Johnson, *The Autobiography*, 12.

31. In a way, though, the protagonist *has* been preoccupied with racial recognition insofar as white racial recognition is often marked by invisibility. As Ruth Frankenberg notes, white people sometimes experience race identity as race privilege, and such identity is often "normalized to the point of invisibility." See Frankenberg, *White Women, Race Matters: The Social Construction of Whiteness* (Minneapolis: University of Minnesota Press, 1993), 179 and elsewhere. So far, the protagonist has in many ways had the privilege of whiteness. That is not to say that he is white, or that people have taken much notice of his whiteness. But the very privilege of *not* engaging in what Kate Evans calls the "emotional work" of marginalized identities has made him an honorary white person until the mirror recognition scene. This term stems from a dissertation in progress by Kate Evans, University of Washington.

32. This is from Hegel's *Jena Realphilosophie* as translated in Williams, *Recognition*, 85.

33. Johnson, *The Autobiography*, 12.

34. Taylor, "The Politics of Recognition," 25.

35. G. W. F. Hegel, *Phenomenology*, 111.

36. Sigmund Freud, "The Uncanny," *The Standard Edition of the Complete Works of Sigmund Freud*, trans. James Strachey with Anna Freud, Alix Strachey, and Alan Tyson (London: Hogarth Press and the Institute of Psycho-Analysis, 1986), Vol. 17, 217–248.

37. Johnson, *The Autobiography*, 11.

38. Franz Fanon, *Black Skins, White Masks* (New York: Grove Weidenfield, 1967), 109.

39. Taylor, "The Politics of Recognition," 25.

40. Fanon, *Black Skins*, 110.

41. This phrase I borrow from Priscilla Wald. See Priscilla Wald, "Becoming 'Colored': The Self-Authorized Language of Difference in Zora Neale Hurston," *American Literary History* 2, no. 1 (1990): 79–100.

42. Jacques Lacan, "The Mirror Stage as Formative of the Function of the I as

Revealed in Psychoanalytic Experience," in *Ecrits: A Selection*, translated by Alan Sheridan (New York: Norton, 1977), 1–7.

43. Honneth, *The Struggle for Recognition*, 162.

44. Honneth, *The Struggle for Recognition*, 165.

45. For a comparison of goods-based versus recognition-based politics, see Fraser, *Justice Interruptus*.

46. Honneth, *The Struggle for Recognition*, 163.

47. Uma Narayan, "Working Together Across Difference: Some Considerations on Emotions and Political Practice," *Hypatia* 3 (1988): 31–47.

The Other Whom I Don't Understand: Confirmation

> Nothing in man—not even his body—is sufficiently stable to serve as the basis for self-recognition or for understanding other men.
>
> —Michel Foucault[1]

> Who am I when *dat* teacher does not know exactly who I am?
>
> —Olivia, interpreted

When Taylor writes that recognition depends upon whether a person does or does not receive "a confining or demeaning or contemptible picture" of herself, there remains the sticky requirement that one has to know the other.[2] The etymology of the word recognition (*recognoscere*, the Latin "to know again") intimates this insistence on knowability, and current uses of the word rely on such a meaning. For example, one entry in the *Oxford English Dictionary* defines recognition as "the action or fact of apprehending a thing under a certain category, or as having a certain character."[3] Recognition has to do with making sense of something, making it fit into a knowable category. Taking this usage seriously, in the hermeneutic sense that the historically imbued connotations of language are part of the historical horizon from which we emerge, it is quite natural that intersubjective recognition should be tied in complicated knots with knowledge-gaining about the self and other.[4]

On the very same page of my dictionary, recognition also means "notice or attention accorded to a thing or person."[5] That is to say, recognition also has to do with affirming another person, with confirming her. It may not be necessary to know a person in order to promote or affirm her as a person. So, while a liberal version of mirror recognition is mainly concerned with instances where knowledge of self yields recognition, what about instances when recognition-as-knowing and recognition-as-self-worth do not overlap? These two meanings of recognition may overlap, but they may not. What if the acknowledgment of an other requires knowledge that is difficult, impossible, or even undesirable to obtain? What might acknowledgment look like if the other does not desire to be known? The separate and distinct entries in my dictionary are emblematic of the importance of teasing out the differences between a knowing recognition and a recognition of unknowability. Whereas a liberal version of mirroring conflates recognizing with knowing, in this chapter I want to examine a non-epistemological redescription of interhuman encounters.

As I stated earlier, Martin Buber is concerned with human encounters in which recognition occurs when the other takes one by surprise. What's more, Buber's conception of the surprise can be fruitfully described as a non-epistemological version of recognition. Buber arrests and augments the Hegelian moment of independence-of-the-other by casting it in terms of a refusal to know.

It might be argued that Buber's position is untenable, and that one can pay "notice or attention" to the other only after the other has been identified. Such a critique misreads Buber because it misses the essential future-looking component of confirmation. Buber is not concerned with confirming what a person is, but what she can become. Buber insists on the sorts of "notice or attention" to the other that actively forestall categorizing and reidentification. Buber's analysis is an existential understanding of future possibility rather than a representational effort to come to terms with what identity has already been. Buber's analysis locates Hegelian independence-of-the-other in the other of the future, and the future is by definition that which we cannot know. As we noted earlier, confirmation has to do with what the other "can become" by means of a recognitive "reaction which cannot be prepared beforehand."[6]

It is because of this future-looking tendency of confirmation that Buber's version of recognition may be practiced in seemingly disparate instances—both when the other *should not* and when he *cannot* be identified. These normative and epistemological aspects of independence are one to Buber. Confirmation is premised on the humanistic precept that the other's future is most important. That future must be confirmed in the realm of the possible instead of the actual.

In this chapter I will elaborate on Martin Buber's confirmative account of recognition, describing more thoroughly its anti-epistemological bent.

I will also utilize and challenge that account. I will utilize it by giving specific educational examples that exemplify confirmation, and I will challenge it by showing how oppressive societal tendencies can infect the practice of confirmation. In Buber's eyes, recognition must be unlinked from an explanation of the value of the other's present position. In my eyes, Buber's confirmation must be subject to scrutiny for its uses, but also examined for its blind spots. One of its main blind spots is the insidious structure of racism that often prestructures the very means that one has available to recognize an other. While Buber quite usefully pinpoints the need for future-looking confirmation, it is dangerous to stay pinned down at the confirmative moment for long. Confirming must not be severed for more than an instant from the workings of power that are constitutive of the encounter.

It is useful to begin fleshing out the work of confirmation by showing how confirmation offers insight into a debate between toleration and liberal recognition, which continues in both educational theory and political philosophy. Insinuating confirmation into this debate serves two purposes: it highlights some of the epistemological assumptions that underwrite usual versions of this debate, and it puts confirmation in stark relief as a third option, an option different from typical understandings of tolerance and recognition, one that does not insist upon an epistemological model of cultural identity. Buber's notion of confirmation is a welcome supplement to epistemological notions of recognition. A discourse of confirmation is useful because it serves as a reminder that privileging *sameness* is not the only alternative to privileging differences that are not completely understood.

CONFIRMATION, TOLERANCE, AND RECOGNITION

Toleration, as it is commonly formulated in political philosophy, is concerned with the consequences of an individual's cultural or religious identity. How can I be tolerant of an other who does not share my belief system? What does it mean to be tolerant of an other even if his or her tolerance of me is limited, to be tolerant of an other whose belief system does not permit him to conform to the tasks that I, as institutional leader (as teacher or as governor, for example), need him to carry out, or to be tolerant of an individual's belief system even if that belief system keeps her from exercising her own individual liberty? These are the sorts of difficult issues that come into play during a conversation about toleration.

John Locke, in his "A Letter Concerning Toleration" of 1689, investigates the issue of tolerance by looking into a particularly heartfelt, if not enthusiastic, type of identity affiliation—religious belief.[7] Following Locke, the tension between state mandates and religious affiliation is a typical instance where toleration is needed. He argues that because religious beliefs are not subject to the will, these beliefs require toleration; that is, because of religious fervor, one cannot change one's religious habits at will. It would be the mark of an unjust government to be intolerant of a citizen's religious practices. A government would have to use coercion to change the religious habits of a person who is vehement about her faith. Tolerance is called for in this case. Even if the state's mandate would liberate the individual from the yoke of religious parochialism, such a mandate must not be carried out. Tolerance, as described by Locke, can be generally defined as *the acknowledgment that a person's religious or cultural horizon is important enough not to be challenged.*[8]

Locke's description of toleration fits in with the political philosophy of liberal individualism. For Locke and the project of liberal individualism at large, one is tolerant of an other mainly because one does not want to interfere with an other's cultural identity; my active support is not key to your sense of identity, and I acknowledge your individual right to be who you are. I will not jump over the fence onto the lawn of your belief system. Locke's version of tolerance is not a matter of bolstering one group or another; it is a matter of noninterference with the habits of individuals. Indeed, the debate on tolerance has generally been bifurcated into two philosophical camps. On one side are the proponents of liberalism, such as Locke, who employ tolerance as a tool for adjusting individual and governmental attitudes in order to deal with the "unfortunate" necessity of cultural or religious affiliation.

Opposed to proponents of "mere" tolerance are those who support a project of recognition, supporters who echo Charles Taylor's dictum that "due recognition is not just a courtesy we owe people. It is a vital human need."[9] As we have seen, the call for liberal recognition makes different claims about the role of cultural horizons in relation to an individual. Instead of seeing cultural identity as a matter of disconnected individuals, where a person of one culture needs to tolerate those of another culture, where one needs to give others space on their side of the fence, the call for recognition, in contrast, maintains that diverse identities need to be reflected positively in society at large. Insiders need recognition from outsiders.

In the public space of schools, for instance, a project of recognition insists that the group identity of the individual needs to be bolstered if that person is to flourish. As noted in the previous chapter, educational multiculturalism can be described in terms of recognition. The connection between multiculturalism and recognition can be seen in an excerpt from an American Association of Colleges of Teacher Education document.

> Multicultural education is education which values cultural pluralism. Multicultural education *rejects the view that schools should merely tolerate cultural pluralism*. Instead, multicultural education affirms that schools should be oriented toward the cultural enrichment of all children and youth through programs rooted to the preservation and extension of cultural alternatives. Multicultural education recognizes cultural diversity as a fact of life in American society, and it affirms that this cultural diversity is a valuable resource that should be preserved and extended.[10]

Multicultural education, as it appears here, is predicated upon a paradigm of liberal recognition and not toleration.

A discourse of liberal recognition makes different claims about the nature of self and identity than does a discourse of tolerance. The self, according to this call for recognition, is not autonomously situated. Instead, the self always looks to others for its sense of identity. Following Hegel, Taylor insists that the self always attains consciousness through an other, and that there is no way of being for humans that is completely autonomous, that the self is dependent on an other as she comes to understand who she is.[11] For the model of recognition that is advocated by Taylor, people need more than noninterference. A person needs a positive reflection by others of his or her group affiliation. Humans need more than to be left alone. The concept of recognition offers a robust picture of people who are imbricated instead of isolated. People live and flourish within what Donna Kerr has called "circuits of recognition."[12]

But liberal recognition does not stand in *unproblematically* for the individualist conception of tolerance. While I do think that recognition offers a more fruitful understanding of identity for educators, I want to challenge even the recognition side of the conversation over tolerance. In fact, whether it be from the advocates of tolerance or from the advocates of recognition, the conversation about toleration that I have just described has a large gap: it assumes a version of cultural identity that is clear and identifiable. It assumes, for example, that a teacher or the classmates of a particular student will be able to bolster the self-image of that student by first naming the culture of that child and will then be able provide a positive representation of that culture for the student. The gap in this conversation shows itself when the cultural identity of the student is not clear to others.

At least three scenarios come to mind wherein the identity of a person might not be available to others and where mirroring might not therefore be forthcoming. First, what if an individual's identity depends upon a discourse that is silenced in hegemonic culture? As Michael Walzer has pointed out, many industrialized nations, such as the United States, have a "regime of tolerance" (and we might likewise say a regime of recognition) that carves out space for a constellation of groups that have either formal or informal protection and are officially afforded at least a modicum of recognition.[13] Such a regime usually consists of a finite number of identity groupings. If one's identity does not fit within a society's "regime," there may not be discursive means by which one can be easily "known." Such is the case in many of our public schools with regard to teachers or students who identify as gay, lesbian, or bisexual.

Second, what if the other is so loathsome that I do not want to mirror him or her? Especially in schools where students arrive with both ethical and unethical habits, how can I want to know an other when I do not consider that other worth knowing?

Third, what if the other is simply outside of the scope of my understanding? What if my own experiences have not given me an opportunity to represent the other in a meaningful way? There will always be others whose language I do not speak, whose customs I do not understand, and whose identity is therefore "un-mirror-able" to me. An other may occupy a distinctive discursive space within a regime of tolerance, or within a regime of recognition, and still be too distant for me to know. In such instances Martin Buber's notion of "confirmation" is particularly useful.

Giving Distance to the Other

In its basic form, the intersubjective encounter theorized by Buber is much the same as Taylor's. For instance, Buber, like Taylor, stresses the dependence of one person on an other. Like Taylor, who insists that people always seek recognition from "the people or society around them,"

Buber argues that people always look to others for recognition. In *The Knowledge of Man*, Buber explains his own version of the encounter as follows:

> Sent forth from the natural domain of species into the hazard of the solitary category, surrounded by the air of a chaos which came into being with him, secretly and bashfully [a person] watches for a Yes which allows him to be and which can come to him only from one human person to another.[14]

Like Taylor, Buber suggests that the self is essentially dependent on an other, that recognition is critical to human flourishing. Buber refers to this human "Yes" as "confirmation."

Buber's theory of confirmation is distinct from Taylor's conception of recognition in one crucial respect, however. Whereas Taylor suggests that the quality of recognition one receives is bound up in whether the other mirrors back "a confining or contemptible picture," Buber's confirmation is based on the assumption that the other is so radically different from oneself that one *cannot* know in advance what to mirror. His theory of the encounter is best distinguished from Taylor's recognitive notion of favorable representation by looking at what Buber terms the "two-fold movement": a movement first of distance and then of relation.

Confirmation cannot begin without the initial movement of distancing. What is distancing? It is precisely an acceptance that the other is essentially unique and unknowable. Buber explains the link between distancing and confirmation as follows: "The person is other, essentially other than myself, and this otherness of his is what I mean, because I mean him; I *confirm* it."[15] Otherness "is constituted as otherness by the event of 'distancing.' "[16] Otherness cannot be confirmed beginning with epistemological approximation. It needs to happen through distancing, through an other's being *other*.

One cannot prepare a "picture" that will serve to confirm an other. Confirming entails acknowledgment of an other who has, as Buber puts it, "a different touch from the regions of existence," a touch that I could not possibly explain or mirror.[17] Maurice Friedman notes, of Buber's confirmation, that one must not "overlook the real 'otherness' of the other person."[18] In Buber's words,

> everything depends so far as human life is concerned, on whether each thinks of the other as the one he is, whether each, that is, with all his desire

to influence the other, nevertheless unreservedly accepts and confirms him in his being this man and in his being made in this particular way.[19]

Buber's theory is a confirmation of radical "alterity" or otherness. Unlike the sort of confirmation one might give another person by empathizing with her, or sharing that person's pain, Buber's confirmation does not come from bridging the gap between self and other. One confirms an other by acknowledging that he or she has a different touch from the regions of existence.

While my reading of Buber highlights the distancing part of Buber's twofold movement, the movement of distancing and relation, I do not mean that Buber's version of self is atomistic. The second part of the twofold movement, relation, is the necessary concomitant of distancing. Though one does not know the other, and cannot know the other, the other still needs confirmation by means of relation. Emphasizing both distance and relation, individuality is not privileged even though distinctness is. That is to say, a confirmative encounter strives for a connection between individuals even if those two individuals cannot know each other cognitively. Buber's dialogic orientation requires both the positing of otherness and the touch.

Because my reading of Buber, as we will see later, is a challenge to those who read Buber with an insistence on community instead of on otherness, let me take a bit of a detour through the historical influences on Buber's thought. I read Buber's confirmative account of the encounter against the backdrop of his experience as a Jewish educator working under the pressure of, and against, Nazi propaganda. As Maurice Friedman notes, Buber carried on a dialogue with otherness in 1930s Germany under the most prejudiced circumstances imaginable.[20] He published accounts of his own Jewish faith and of his worldview of the twofold movement of distance and relation during a time when the German population at large was turning to a racial "solution." I see Buber's work on unknowability as a necessary political alternative to eugenic sensibilities that categorize people according to cultural identities.

Maurice Friedman supports the parallels between Buber's refusal of fascist stereotyping and Buber's resistance to attempts at knowing the other. Friedman writes that during the 1930's,

Buber introduced a decisive development in his own philosophical anthropology which was also clearly his own understanding of how such an evil as Nazism could come to be. Man is not radically anything, Buber claimed. He is "the crystallized potentiality of existence . . . in its factual limitation." . . . The action of the human being is unforeseeable in its nature and extent; for man is "the centre of all surprise in the world."[21]

Identity, instead of being limited to steadfast representations of *who I am*, needs to be established by the surprise of *who I turn out to be*. Buber's "centre of all surprise" refutes such deterministic notions as *Folk*, and it questions the predefined hierarchies embodied in such notions. As Friedman points out, Buber objects to the Nazi tendency of speaking of "*the* Jewish doctor, *the* Jewish lawyer, and *the* Jewish merchant."[22] Buber's "centre of surprise" is suspicious of the ways that group identification can go murderously awry. It is at once a historical reaction to fascism and a linchpin of Buber's notion of confirmation.

Classroom Confirmation

To begin looking through a confirmative lens onto classroom recognition, it is helpful to consider how teachers are sometimes called upon to be "present" to their students during circumstances that do not favor mirroring and knowing the other. Recently an art teacher told me of an experience that shows how an encounter can sometimes call for unknowability.

Ms. Call was teaching a unit on graphic arts to her junior high school students. The unit came just after a unit they had done on figure sculptures, and it came before one on watercolor painting. On the first day of the unit, the students spent a class period leafing through magazines, finding advertisements that they found appealing, and sharing the contents with the class while Ms. Call explained some of the processes that graphic artists use to come up with their final products. On the second day of class, the students were to use the ideas they had gleaned from the discussion and from their observations to draw what Ms. Call termed a "layout" for their own advertisements. On the third day, Ms. Call asked if anyone had a layout to share.

Tommy, one of Ms. Calls more prolific art students, had spent all of the second day sketching like mad. On the third day, Ms. Call noticed that he was gaining quite a bit of attention from the students around him. He was showing the students what he was drawing. There were murmurs and snickers. Ms. Call knew from the hushed tones that Tommy was up to something she might not approve of. She was a seasoned teacher, though, and was not flustered by junior high school antics. She knew when to lie back and let the latest intrigue blow over, and when to bring in a firm hand of discipline. What's more, Ms. Call believed in artistic freedom. She was not about to actively police the content of student art unless its content was flaunted, or unless the content put her in a position that forced an ethical choice.

She used a gentle approach to the snickers as she always did: "Tommy, is there something you would like to share with the whole class?"

Tommy seemed to be inflated by urgings of his classmates. They were nodding their heads, saying, "Show her, Tommy. Come on, show her."

He held up his layout for Ms. Call to see. "Well, Ms. Call, this is my magazine advertisement. It's for a new machine. I call it the 'Jew Burner 2000.' "

Ms. Call was quick to respond. She went right over to face Tommy, and put one hand on his shoulder. She looked him in the eye and said, "Do you know that I'm Jewish, Tommy? Do you realize what you just said you are going to do to *me*?"

Ms. Call's response was a powerful example of being present for the other, of recognizing him, even though Tommy's actions were not worthy of positive acknowledgment. Her response was sensitive to a certain recognitive need for human affirmation; hence, the touch on the shoulder. Yet, she did not go so far as to reflect Tommy in a positive way. She did not dignify his loathsome actions with any sort of response that might "reflect" those actions positively. Instead, she tended to a human need for affirmation while challenging the way Tommy wanted to be *known*. She kept a certain distance from condoning who Tommy was at that moment, from claiming to know or understand his position, but at the same time she kept a certain closeness, by means of the touch, to Tommy's need for an other's response.

I had similar experiences as a high school teacher, though I don't remember responding in such a productive way. Perhaps I have not been able to use an unknowing form of recognition as did Ms. Call because acknowledgment is so often inflected by what kind of picture one has of the other. It's hard to confirm what one disapproves of. How does one acknowledge an other who is loathsome and therefore "un-mirror-able"? Ms. Call was able to do so. She acknowledged Tommy by means of her touch even though she wasn't able to understand his viewpoint. She granted him recognition even though she did not condone that part of Tommy about which she had knowledge.

Buber's notion of confirmation highlights the threshold position that one must be able to negotiate in instances such as the one faced by Ms. Call. When one is caught between the Scylla of acknowledging that the other's position is somehow admirable and the Charybdis of condemning the other, a confirmative stance speaks to instances when educators cannot rely on a neat curricular model that will foster the self-recognition of students, when educators need something different from epistemological access to student identity. The threshold position of distance and presence is an essential tool in circumstances where an educator must be humanly present by virtue of her institutional role as caretaker but must also claim distance from the unethical positions of particular students. Some students come to school with positions that need not be reflected in the classroom. The fact remains, though, that they are in school. And they are there with us.

Confirmation and Queer Theory

With Buber's formulation of unknowability in mind, I turn to queer theory. I do so because Buber's notion of the unknowable other intersects with some of the theoretical underpinnings of queer theory.[23] For example, queer theory questions the usefulness of notions of stable, essential identities. It asks such questions as these: Is it beneficial to solidify identity categories, or is categorizing repressive to those who do not want to be pigeonholed into one particular identity? Is there such a stable thing as "the homosexual," or is homosexuality simply a relational placemarker in the heterosexist matrix? If homosexuality itself is already defined within the prejudiced understandings of heterosexist culture, then isn't it more politically empowering to blur the seemingly "obvious" categories of sexual identities? The heterosexist matrix creates a homosexual/heterosexual binary that naturalizes heterosexuality at the expense of homosexuality. Queer theory is a way to question such a pathologizing binary.[24]

Given current struggles of queer people to forge identities that are not subject to regulatory norms, it is important to question whether it is even possible for gays, lesbians, and bisexuals to be well recognized within the heterosexist matrix. It may possibly be more empowering for gays, lesbians, and bisexuals not to be "known" as such. It may be more empowering to destabilize the very categories of gay and straight. Ellspeth Probyn, advocating a queer sensibility, describes the individual as "a singularity that cannot be posed in advance and that must not be posited as negating other singularities."[25] Queer theory insists that it is more politically fruitful to destabilize identity categories than it is to solidify them.[26]

In addition to questioning the political usefulness of stable identity categories, queer theorists have underscored the use-value of being out instead of assuming that being out is always the most liberating position. Contrary to the social logic of recognition, queer theorists would argue "baring one's soul" needs to be used tactically.[27] Because it cannot be assumed that heterosexist norms will even allow a friendly discursive space for recognition of nonheterosexist subjectivities, there is no guarantee that being recognized as a gay, lesbian, or bisexual will be a positive move in any way. Baring one's soul may in fact reify a homosexual identity that, within heterosexual culture, is taken to be a negation of heterosexuality. Baring one's soul for recognition as homosexual may be quite inimical to the proliferation of identity possibilities central to queer activism.

To put it simply, recognitive struggles assume that everyone wants to be, or needs to be, "out." The struggle for recognition, as it is generally conceived by adherents such as Charles Taylor, requires one to say what one wants to be recognized for. Recognition requires that I wear on my lapel the authentic *me* for whom I seek recognition. It insists on an identity of up-frontness. Charles Taylor, using a Gadamerian metaphor to theorize contemporary identity politics, says that "recognizing difference, like self-choosing, requires a horizon of significance."[28] Such a horizon requires the ability to articulate an identity position in order to be recognized. Michel Foucault calls this phenomenon of "having-to-say" the "speaker's benefit."[29] He notes that modern notions of self have been shaped by the religious and social-scientific models of baring one's soul. Thus, we usually feel empowered when we can "tell all" and when we receive recognition of what we have said. A liberal notion of recognition that is based on such a publicly sayable understanding of self can be to the detriment of queer politics.

Confirmation, Education, and Character

In light of the above discussion, Buber's own educational philosophy looks similar to an educational theory that queer theory would embrace. Buber begins his essay "The Education of Character" with this statement:

"Education worthy of the name is essentially education of character."[30] The phrase *education of character* indicates the sort of teaching that is done in moments that are not foreseen. "Only in his whole being, in all his spontaneity," writes Buber, "can the educator truly affect the whole being of his pupil."[31] The educator shows an ability to be "wholly alive" in an unscripted way.[32] I say "unscripted" here to mean a teacher-as-character who remains spontaneous to whatever possibility a student brings forth. A wholly alive, spontaneous teacher-as-character is prepared to acknowledge the student outside the parameters of what is slated to be taught on any particular day and, I would queerly add, outside of the parameters of the homosexual/heterosexual matrix.

To give an example of the sort of situation in which the teacher-as-character teaches, Buber offers the following scenario.

> The teacher who is for the first time approached by a boy with somewhat defiant bearing, but with trembling hands visibly opened-up and fired by a daring hope, who asks him what is the right thing in a certain situation—for instance, whether in learning that a friend has betrayed a secret entrusted to him one should call him to account or be content with entrusting no more secrets to him—the teacher to whom this happens realizes that this is the moment to make the first conscious step towards education of character.[33]

It is not too much of a stretch to say that this "secret entrusted to him" could have been a secret of love, perhaps a love of secret. In this instance, the teacher can show her or his own "character" by accepting the student "before desiring to influence him."[34] Because the situation is unforeseen, there is the possibility that the teacher can shed the cumbersome teaching plan and be fully present. As Buber says, "it is not the educational intention but it is the meeting that is educationally fruitful."[35] Secrets may be as important to confirm as "out"-right descriptions of identities.

There is another way to interpret the "education of character," as the education of students who might themselves become "great characters." As Buber puts it, the educator's "real goal which, once he has well recognized it and well remembers it, will influence all his work, is the great character."[36] The student-as-character exhibits the same qualities as the teacher-as-character. The main difference is that one does not know when the student will be called upon to exhibit the spontaneous call of confirmation. Whereas the teacher-as-character has as his or her goal to step out of curricular simplifications and into spontaneity, the student-as-character will have a different role to step out of. The various venues in which the student-as-character might practice her spontaneity are not yet in view. The student-as-character may be a bus driver or a salesperson. In whatever role she takes up, or whether she is called upon to confirm an other while still a student, her goal will be to practice unforeseen acknowledgment of the other.

Buber explains what the student-as-character will be like:

> The great character can be conceived neither as a system of maxims nor as a system of habits. It is peculiar to him to act from the whole of his substance. That is, it is peculiar to him to react in accordance with the uniqueness of every situation which challenges him as an active person. Of course there are all sorts of similarities in different situations. . . . But what is untypical in the particular situation remains unnoticed and unanswered.[37]

The student-as-character, like the teacher-as-character, will be ready to step out of a preconceived notion of how to act according to this or that script. He or she will rely upon the spontaneity of human presence.

The education of character, in both its teacher and student versions, provides an example of educational confirmation in practice. Buber's description begins to answer the question "If not mirror recognition, then what?" The education of character points to the way confirmation might be practiced in schools. For Buber, the key terms for the education of character, and for confirmation, are *presence* and *particular situation*. A practice of educational confirmation would encourage specific, unmediated encounters between self and other. Such encounters would not rely upon a "hoard of established maxims and habits."[38] Preconceived notions about the other detract from the possibility of an I–Thou presence with an other just as they detract from the particular situation in which the encounter happens.[39] The confirming encounter, on the other hand, is a face-to-face event that insists on its own uniqueness. Such an event requires an otherness that might be "out" or might not be.

Meshing queer theory and Buber's education of character as I have done may seem like encouraging a chance meeting. That is only so if one allows the current label of "character," a mantra embraced by conservatives to effect a reversion to oppressive ways of old, to take hold. Buber's notion of character is quite foreign to the rightist claim that there is a certain moral code that one must live by in order to be a great character. Buber's character is not at all prescriptive; it is ideologically in sync with the same queer sensibilities that rightist claims to "character" abhor. There is currently a performative contradiction that resounds from the very utterance of the phrase *education of character;* the phrase unfortunately undercuts its own intent. Given the politically charged bias of the more popular variations of "character education," Buber's education of character is perhaps better described as an "education of uncharacter," because Buber is more concerned with confirming the uncharacteristic than relying on any steadfast notions of character.

CONFIRMATION AS MENTAL IMAGING VERSUS CONFIRMATION AS PRESENCE

With the theoretical and historical underpinnings of Buber's center of surprise in mind, I want to point out that some conceptions of educational confirmation have done a disservice to Buber's thought. Past conceptions have assimilated Buber's notion of confirmation into a model of mental imaging.

For example, Nel Noddings has advocated an understanding of confirmation as one of "the three great means of nurturing the ethical ideal."[40] Since Noddings's work is prominent in educational philosophy, I want to clarify Noddings's use of confirmation in contrast to my own. The version of confirmation I am dealing with in this work shares little with Noddings's. While Noddings derives her conception of confirmation from Buber, my own understanding of confirmation is diametrically opposed to Noddings's.

Noddings describes confirmation as follows.

> When we attribute the best possible motive consonant with reality to the cared-for, we confirm him; that is, we reveal to him an attainable image of himself that is lovelier than that manifested in his present act.[41]

Confirmation, according to Noddings, requires an attribution of motive. It is a mirroring-back to the other the best (the "loveliest") that he or she could be. Confirmation means embracing an other as he or she is and then finding something admirable in that person. "As a result," says Noddings, "he may find strength to become even more admirable. He is confirmed."[42] This is an epistemological understanding of confirmation. One tries to know what an other might possibly be like in the future. In particular, one only looks for admirable knowledge about an other.

The version of confirmation that Noddings offers is an interesting addition to Noddings's own discussion of the ethics of caring. For Noddings, confirmation serves as an antidote to the "masculine" way of cultivating ethical or intellectual standards upon some sort of objectified grid. Grades, for Noddings, are such an objectifying grid. Noddings uses confirmation in a discussion of educational grading and evaluation. Evaluation is objectifying and "masculine"-izing, but confirmation is a more caring and "feminine" approach to grading. The caring teacher will use confirmation instead of evaluation:

> The teacher who values her subject will be concerned with his [the student's] own work. She seeks to *confirm* him in his intellectual life as well as in his ethical life . . . neither has a need for grades.[43]

For Noddings, grading by confirming would grow "out of what may be a mixture of feelings and motives."[44] Within Noddings's educational ethics of caring, confirmation is understood as a means for avoiding objectification.

In the narrow sense of avoiding objectification, Noddings's version of confirmation does jibe with Buber's confirmation of otherness. However, to the extent that Noddings invokes Buber's confirmation as an alternative (albeit more personable) way to evaluate student progress, she does not capture his anti-epistemological sense of confirmation. Noddings's version of confirmation has little to do with Buber's insight into the utter otherness entailed in confirmation.

I take issue with this educational conception of confirmation not only because it does not ring true to Buber's thought, but because it diminishes the very aspect of Buber's educational work that is so unique and incisive. Confirmation, as Buber describes it, happens "in a strictly ontological sense."[45] Becoming admirable may be a by-product of confirmation, but confirmation does not start with such an attribution.[46] Instead of searching out and acknowledging what is good and admirable in an other, confirmation, as I read Buber, begins when one recognizes the other in his or her unknowability. The upshot of confirmation should not be anticipated.

Perhaps the best way to distinguish confirmation from searching out what is good and admirable in a person is to emphasize the passiveness and unpreparedness that go along with Buber's notion of confirmation.

For Buber, confirmation can only come after I have let the other happen to me.[47] In order to confirm an other, in order to be present, one cannot know in advance how to approach that person in a given situation. One cannot be prepared with something admirable to attribute to that person. The other must happen to me as a surprise, an unknown, first; only subsequently can confirmation follow. As Buber explains,

> Except in general terms and overall predictions, one's resources are only known in the situation itself. This is because one's resources, one's potentialities, do not simply inhere in one as a part of one's makeup, but are called out of one in response to what meets and demands one in this hour.[48]

My confirmation of an other does not consist of attributing anything specific to her. It can only occur when the other happens to me, and in such a way that I couldn't expect.

In sum, by assimilating confirmation to positive mental imaging, Noddings takes away the provocative import of Buber's work. Most provocative, I think, within Buber's conception of confirmation, is this: How we understand one another, or what exactly we say, is not so important. The one confirming must be willing to make a gesture, or take a stance, of relatedness. Such a gesture or stance depends not on affirming the content of the relation; it depends rather on a willingness to stand fast while confirming the other's otherness. Most important is that we are present to one another, that we stand in an I–Thou relationship.

What about Humanistic Claims?

At this point it is timely to say something about the humanisms of Charles Taylor and Martin Buber, and about my own. It is timely because the preceding account of Buber's confirmation may seem to imply that Buber knows something about human beings that other people don't. Certainly both Taylor and Buber have a certain view of what it means to be human, and their humanistic views guide their understandings of the encounter. As I have mentioned, Taylor assumes that human beings are historically situated to seek recognition. In a manner that is fundamentally Hegelian, Taylor theorizes that humans need to act in certain ways with each other because human culture has progressed to the point where our interaction must be recognitive.[49] Taylor's historical humanism is particularly apparent in instances where he claims to know why humans demand things like curricular representation—it's because humans simply are that way these days: humans are recognizing beings.

Likewise, when Buber describes the twofold movement, he describes it as if that is simply the way people are. For Buber, human beings are fundamentally unique, and they are fundamentally relational. Therefore, it is the duty and the ability of every person to practice confirmation. When he claims that "the basis of man's life with man is twofold," he claims to know specifics about the human condition.[50] He seems to be telling a truth about people in general.

In keeping with my own pragmatic orientation, I interpret neither Taylor nor Buber as having objective knowledge that speaks to what it means to be human. Both Taylor and Buber offer detailed accounts of acknowledgment that follow directly from their own views of the intersubjective person. I see their work not as proof that humans are like this or that, nor as proof that humans need this or that sort of acknowledgment, but as providing useful lenses for the encounter between self and other. My own humanism is thinner than either Taylor's or Buber's insofar as my only claim is that interhuman encounters are important enough to need sustained attention. As I mentioned in the introduction, my experience as a teacher has taught me that interpersonal acknowledgment is a phenomenon that needs educational attention.

By arguing that Noddings's use of Buber takes away the provocative import of Buber's work, I do not mean to say that Buber got human beings right and Noddings did not. I mean rather that my interpretation of Buber is a useful lens onto human encounters in certain ways that Noddings's is not. Buber's own texts, as well as the historical circumstances under which Buber theorized human encounters, bear out the importance of the center of surprise. In particular, Buber's confirmation of unknowability helps to make sense of how one can acknowledge the loathsome, the unavailable, and the unfamiliar.

CONFIRMATION, EDUCATION, AND THE RACIST MATRIX

It is with this conception of the encounter as confirmation that I read Ernest Gaines's novel *A Lesson before Dying*.[51] Educational confirmation is the central theme in Gaines's text. He writes of Jefferson, a young black man in the South of the United States, who has been accused of robbing a liquor store and murdering its owner. During the robbery, Jefferson was

in the company of two other men who were both killed, leaving no witnesses to testify that Jefferson did not help commit the murder. Jefferson
is convicted and sentenced to death. He is convicted within the racist cultural matrix of a southern town where blacks are assumed guilty unless
innocence is proven. He is convicted in what legal theorist Patricia Williams calls an "unconscious restructuring of burdens of proof into burdens of white over black."[52] In other words, in the absence of concrete
evidence, it is assumed, in the largely white legal system, that this black
man is guilty by virtue of only circumstantial evidence.

The story unfolds with Jefferson secluded in his jail cell. Grant Wiggins,
the town's schoolteacher, is asked by some of the townspeople to visit
him in jail. They want him to give Jefferson one last "lesson before
dying." Giving Jefferson a lesson before dying means, among other
things, giving him his dignity before he is put to death. Jefferson's aunt,
for example, tells Wiggins that he needs to "make a man" out of Jefferson.
She doesn't want to see him die like a coward. Nor does she want him to
die without committing his soul to Jesus. Interestingly, Wiggins is presumed to be the most likely candidate to teach Jefferson such a lesson
because of his stature as a schoolteacher. Even though he is not a religious
person, the townspeople want Wiggins-as-teacher to give Jefferson this
one last "lesson" of religious faith and human dignity. Wiggins resists
going to the jail but is persuaded by his aunt and Jefferson's grandmother
to do so.

Gaines's text theorizes confirmation because the text deals precisely
with the spontaneous and unknowable moment that must surround any
attempt at confirmation. Jefferson's condition is quite unknowable to
Wiggins. Wiggins has very little knowledge of this young man. While
Wiggins did attend the trial, Jefferson has no knowledge of what is in
Wiggins's heart—Jefferson knows only what Wiggins stands accused of.
He has not been a close friend to Wiggins, and it is doubtful that Wiggins
and he could establish much of a formal student/teacher relationship.
Even though Jefferson was a student in the past, it is apparent that teachers have never before "reached" Jefferson in an educational sense; his
spelling and diction indicate that he learned little while at school. As
readers, we know this because Wiggins eventually gives Jefferson a journal in which to write down his thoughts. Jefferson's writing is barely understandable. Moreover, Jefferson will barely speak to Wiggins. What
Wiggins says about people in general certainly applies to the lack of
knowledge he has about Jefferson: "Who knows what somebody else is

thinking? They say one thing, they may be thinking about something else—who can tell?"[53] Wiggins is supposed to teach him faith in Jesus and supposed to teach him to "be a man," yet the gap in worldviews between Jefferson and his former teacher is formidable.

The confirmative bent of this text is further revealed by its dramatic setting. Gaines's text is contoured with an architecture of unknowability. The jail in which Jefferson is incarcerated is literally and metaphorically a place of otherness. Barred, locked, kept off-limits to all but a few visitors, the jail keeps Jefferson concealed from the outside world just as Jefferson's personality is concealed from the reader and from Wiggins. The jail itself is an architectural reminder of the question Wiggins poses about people in general: "Who knows what somebody else is thinking?"[54] The jail is a physical manifestation of the unknowability of Jefferson's psychological condition. It is a physical reminder that Jefferson's circumstances call for confirmation of the other and not knowledge of him, that whatever there is that is knowable about Jefferson is as inscrutable to Wiggins as Jefferson's jail cell is to the general public.

As readers of this text, we know as little about Jefferson as the characters do. We know little of his personality and his life experiences prior to the conviction. We do not even know whether he committed the murder. His actions while in prison are bizarre: we do not know why Jefferson refuses to eat with utensils once he is imprisoned, we do not know why he refuses to wash, and we do not know why he refuses to talk. As a reader, I am struck by the unknowability of this young man.

Not only does the unknowable quality of Wiggins's encounter with Jefferson theorize confirmation, but their encounter is also confirmative by virtue of the *unanticipatible* nature of each prison visit.[55] Wiggins does not force any particular teaching onto Jefferson. Instead, he confirms Jefferson in the particular circumstances that crop up during each visit. Wiggins confirms Jefferson in unexpected ways that are not particularly teacherlike. He gives Jefferson a radio to listen to the jazz he enjoys. He brings Jefferson food without insisting that he eat it. He encourages Jefferson to write his own thoughts in a diary, but he does not ask Jefferson to improve his writing style, nor to write with proper grammar. Wiggins's visits, and his seemingly unteacherlike attention to the needs of Jefferson, are reminiscent of what Buber calls the "other half" of education: "This almost imperceptible, most delicate approach, the raising of a finger, or a questioning glance, is the other half of what happens in education."[56]

Through a series of prison visits from Wiggins, Jefferson is indeed confirmed. By virtue of what Maurice Friedman has called a by-product of the I–Thou encounter, Jefferson gains voice and confidence even though he is soon to be put to death. By the end of the novel, Jefferson writes to Wiggins with a renewed sense of self. "good by mr wigin," Jefferson's journal reads, "tell them im strong."[57]

Yet Gaines's text also adds something more than a living example of Buber's confirmation. Emphasizing a political edge to confirmation that is still within the parameters of Buber's project, Gaines's text shows how an event of confirmation can produce political knowledge out of unknowability. As the novel progresses, it is evident that Jefferson's status as innocent or guilty is unknowable mainly because racism precludes Jefferson's case from being tried fairly. Because of the assumption that a young black man is guilty in this southern town, we simply do not know whether Jefferson committed the murder. A shroud of racism is draped thickly over the entire event. Even if Jefferson *has* committed the murder, it is difficult to untangle what might be Jefferson's own fault from what might have been the fault of the social and economic conditions in a town where blacks are unabashedly oppressed. Racial injustice itself lends unknowability to Jefferson's circumstances.

Using confirmation as a lens through which we view Gaines's narrative, the novel's main source of tension and ambiguity lies precisely on the flip side of an unknowing confirmation. Jefferson's situation as a black man who is presumed (without witnesses) to be guilty and who is held in his death-row cell, is a synecdoche for the racist matrix at large. The smaller cell can be taken for the larger society. On one side, then, the novel is about confirmation of Jefferson, pure and simple. It is a matter of one person's presence with another. On the other side, though, the very circumstances that set up such an instance of confirmation were themselves imbued by a historical trajectory of racism. Ironically, the unexpectedness of confirmation is only possible within a cultural matrix of racism that one comes to expect in such a prejudicial atmosphere.

Gaines's text theorizes that confirmation may very well be circumstanced by structural injustices such as racism, and that it is wrong to overlook the possibility that confirmation may actually be more than an encounter between two individuals. It is an encounter between two individuals who are involved in history. *A Lesson before Dying* reminds us how confirmation is sometimes facilitated by the historically imbued identity categories that a willful act of confirmation might initially suggest that we bracket. Even if it is not racism per se that underwrites an act of confirmation, Gaines's text serves as a reminder that the chances that confirmation can take place in a vacuum are slim. The story of Jefferson is a clear reminder that one confirms an other within the constraints of historicity.

Gaines's text offers another gloss on confirmation that is a bit more subtle: it shows that it is sometimes through efforts at confirmation that one becomes aware of one's own historicity. The I–Thou encounter can reveal historical attitudes, behaviors, dispositions, and oppressions that are simply not going to be confirmed away. As *A Lesson before Dying* makes clear, it is sometimes precisely the confirming encounter that accentuates our awareness of oppression. Sometimes, the confirming encounter itself emphasizes the historical conditions of confirmation. Or, to go back to the previous analysis of the Wiggins–Jefferson encounter as confirmation, let me add a gloss to what has already been said: During Wiggins's jail visits to his former student, there is unknowability and unanticipatibility, but there is also the mystifying specter of racism that will not go away. The event of confirmation between Jefferson and Wiggins highlights the cultural matrix of racism that makes their encounter necessary in the first place. A second by-product of the confirmative encounter in this novel is that it encourages an interrogation of the racist circumstances that make such a confirmative encounter available in the first place.

Gaines's text highlights in a palpable way what Hans-Georg Gadamer has explained in philosophical and linguistic terms: "there is no societal reality, with all its concrete forces, that does not bring itself to representation in a consciousness that is linguistically articulated."[58] Historical realities will themselves be manifested within encounters, within communication. Through genuine experience, through the encounter with a Thou, one can gain insight into the constraints of historical reality. Gadamer says that historical conditions, restraints, and traditions are likely to be emphasized in the I–Thou encounter. "Tradition is a genuine partner in dialogue, and we belong to it, as does the I with a Thou."[59] As James Risser puts it, "the I–Thou is not a subject-to-subject relation as a 'mysterious communion of souls,' but simply a participating, a sharing in meaning. This sharing is a sharing in tradition."[60] Gaines's literary presentation of confirmation echoes Gadamer's sentiments that the I–Thou encounter is a sharing of tradition; Gaines highlights how insidious tradition can be.

Gaines insists on a gloss to the unknowing quality of confirmation that I stressed earlier, showing that confirmation can actually be an event of meaning-making. Gaines reverses the anti-epistemological trend of unanticipatible confirmation, showing that confirmation is also a way of knowing. In scenarios of confirmation such as Gaines presents, it is not only the unknowable "particular situation" that is significant. Significant also is the social injustice that such a "particular situation" can make apparent. *A Lesson before Dying* illustrates that confirmation can also promote an unanticipated understanding, but the confirmation that Gaines presents in his text does not yield an "un-whole" mode of understanding, to borrow Buber's word. Gaines's confirmation is not a gaining of knowledge in some precategorized way. Through the unanticipatible encounter, the cultural matrix that makes confirmation possible in the first place is accentuated and more thoroughly understood.

Let me emphasize the shortcomings of confirmation as an educational practice. Because Buber's movement of distancing and relating has important implications for the practice of recognizing students and for putting identity-based judgments on hold long enough to "stick with" the essential human need for recognition, and though Buber's project of confirmation is clearly more profound than simple attentiveness to the most "lovely" aspects of student identity, he simply does not consider to a great enough extent the institutional and societal oppressions that often support intersubjective meetings. It matters not only that two souls can meet in a prison; it matters also the reasons they are forced to meet there in the first place. If a confirmative project is to be more than a meeting of two souls who acknowledge distance and practice relation, the oppressive situations that often govern meetings that take place in such institutions as prisons and schools must be taken into account. They must be acknowledged and ameliorated through social activism in ways that a "pure" Buberian project of confirmation fails to support.

CONFIRMATION, PRESENCE, AND SCHOOL ACTIVISM

If Gaines's story shows a confirmative event that reveals, without changing, a culture of racism, my own experience as a white teacher advising a school group called Students and Teachers Against Racism (STAR) reminds me of the possibility for an agenda of social justice that is guided by confirmative encounters. Our group met biweekly for a few years and was composed of junior high school students from various racial and ethnic backgrounds. The students who attended this group did so voluntarily after school. Students came for socializing, as happens especially in junior high groups. They also came for the opportunity to voice their concerns and take action about racism at school. We made antiracist posters to hang up around school. We had sleep-overs where play and dance were mingled with serious talk about how to combat racism in everyday life. We organized school assemblies that were intended to combat racism.

To a person, these junior high students could remember specific instances of racism that compelled them to come to such a group. Each student had either been the object of a racist act or had witnessed a particular racist incident that involved a close friend or family member. I would not say that these students had a particular cultural identity that needed to be acknowledged. Many of these students were not particularly interested in the curriculum of recognizing diversity that the school had to offer. I know this because I taught some of these same students in my English class. Many of the students in our group did not choose to participate in classroom activities that were ostensibly created with the goal of promoting recognition of every culture. Many of these students needed to experience recognition not as part of an abstract lesson but as a working part of their lives.[61] At STAR, students gained recognition through mutual presence. Buber's notion of confirmation reminds us not to forget the importance of such unanticipatible interhuman instances of presence.

My point is that confirmation is a useful way to think about the recognition that is afforded to students in person-to-person encounters, especially when it comes to encounter groups that promote cultural activism. The presence and interhuman interaction of encounter groups is just as important as the more formal, classroom-based ways of promoting cultural recognition. Groups such as STAR should not be construed as somehow quasi-scholastic simply because students come to dance and make friends. Rather, such recognition-as-confirmation is a matter of serious educational import. It falls under the same rubric as curricular efforts to promote multicultural recognition through curricular representation.

I do not mean to say that after-school groups are the only place that a relation of presence should occur. On the contrary, one aim of this work is to show that the classroom as a public space is an important venue for encounters with the other. While our STAR group did meet after classroom hours, our group should serve as a model for the type of presence that could well happen within the official school day.

Unfortunately, the I–Thou encounter of presence is too often separated out by educators as something distinct from curricular means of fostering recognition. At least at the junior high school where I advised this STAR group, there was a tendency to think of an after-school group such as ours as sort of a surrogate private space. That is to say, STAR, because it was an encounter group, was not part of the "official" curriculum. It was, in fact, run either by adjuncts (such as counselors whose role was that of "support") or by teachers (such as myself, who were considered to have their own agenda that was most appropriately pursued after school). Such a mapping-out of school space is wrong. It serves to relegate the student voice, student empowerment, and student recognition that come from I–Thou encounters to an annex of "real" education.

Buber's confirmation serves as a reminder that such mapping is fundamentally contradictory and uneducative. Buber's insistence on presence is an incisive reminder that recognition may not always be fostered at the level of textual learning. The unknowable and surprising aspects of human encounters are integral to intersubjective recognition. In order to foster recognition in the public space of school, these aspects must be fostered within relationships of presence. A major aspect of recognition is presence with the other, whether or not one "learns about" the other. This means that experiencing the other is as important as knowledge of the other, and that interpersonal confirmation is fundamental to recognition in the classroom. Only with face-to-face experiences between self and other can the unanticipatible nature of selves be confirmed. The classroom should be a public space of confirmation between self and other.

It should also be noted, though, that representation and presence will not guarantee that recognition will be attained. In the next chapter, I will look at the possibility that both positive representation and confirmative presence can still lead to misrecognition. Recognition not only acknowledges subjects, but it also subjects the one recognized to predecided ways of being.

NOTES

1. Michel Foucault, "Nietzsche, Genealogy, History," in *Michel Foucault: Language, Counter-Memory, Practice: Selected Essays and Interviews*, edited by D. F. Bouchard (New York: Cornell University Press, 1977), 153.

2. Charles Taylor, "The Politics of Recognition," in *Multiculturalism: Examining the Politics of Recognition*, edited by Amy Gutman (Princeton, N.J.: Princeton University Press), 25.

3. *The Compact Edition of the Oxford English Dictionary* (Oxford: Oxford University Press, 1971), 2441.

4. See, for example, Hans-Georg Gadamer's "On the Scope and Function of Hermeneutical Reflection," in *Hermeneutics and Modern Philosophy*, edited by Brice R. Wachterhauser (Albany: SUNY Press, 1986). Or, look at Gadamer's *Truth and Method* where he argues that "Being that can be understood is language." (New York: Continuum, 1994), 474.

5. *Oxford English Dictionary*, 2441.

6. Martin Buber, *Between Man and Man* (New York: Collier Books), 61, 114.

7. John Locke, *A Letter Concerning Toleration* (Buffalo, N.Y.: Prometheus Books, 1990).

8. For the purposes of this discussion on tolerance, recognition, and confirmation, I will be using the term "cultural" to signify a broad range of identity horizons, including gender, religion, sexuality, race, ethnicity, and class. This is a generalizing move that works in this particular discussion because epistemological ways of being known are at play with each of these identity horizons.

9. Taylor, "Politics of Recognition," 26.

10. Cited in Cameron McCarthy, "After the Canon," in *Race, Identity and Representation in Education*, edited by Cameron McCarthy and Warren Crichlow (New York: Routledge, 1993), 291, italics mine.

11. G. W. F. Hegel, *Phenomenology of Spirit*, translated by A. V. Miller (New York: Oxford University Press), section 4.

12. See Donna Kerr's use of this phrase in "Toward a Democratic Rhetoric of Schooling," in *The Public Purpose of Education and Schooling*, edited by John I. Goodlad and Timothy J. McMannon (San Francisco: Jossey-Bass, 1997), 73–83. Kerr's terminology here builds on the work of Jessica Benjamin, *The Bonds of Love: Psychoanalysis, Feminism, and the Problem of Domination* (New York: Pantheon, 1988).

13. Michael Walzer, *On Toleration* (New Haven, Conn.: Yale University Press, 1997).

14. Buber, *Knowledge of Man* (London: George Allen & Unwin, 1965), 71.

15. Buber, *Knowledge of Man*, 61.

16. Buber, *Knowledge of Man*, 60.

17. Buber, *Between Man and Man*, 61–62.

18. Maurice Friedman, *The Confirmation of Otherness: In Family, Community, and Society* (New York: Pilgrim Press, 1973), 30.

19. Buber, *Knowledge of Man*, 69.

20. Here I am emphasizing Maurice Friedman's account in *Martin Buber's Life and Work: The Middle Years 1923–1945* (New York: Dutton, 1983).

21. Friedman, *The Middle Years*, 192.

22. Friedman, *The Middle Years*, 185.

23. While "queer theory" is certainly an unstable signifier, and should be, I am

referring here to a queer theory based on these texts, among others: Judith Butler, *Gender Trouble* (New York: Routledge, 1990); Judith Butler, *Excitable Speech: A Politics of the Performative* (New York: Routledge, 1997); Ellspeth Probyn, *Outside Belongings* (New York: Routledge, 1996); Eve Sedgwick, *Epistemology of the Closet* (Berkeley: University of California Press, 1990); Annamarie Jagose, *Queer Theory: An Introduction* (New York: New York University Press, 1997); and, chapter 1 of Nancy Fraser, *Justice Interruptus: Critical Reflections on the "PostSocialist" Condition* (New York: Routledge, 1997) offers a good summary of queer politics.

24. See, for example, Butler, *Gender Trouble*, 77.

25. Probyn, *Outside Belongings*, 42.

26. See Nancy Fraser's summary of queer politics in chapter 1 of *Justice Interruptus*.

27. I am thinking here especially of Butler's affirmation of parody as opposed to authenticity. Butler's conception of performativity in *Gender Trouble*, 136, challenges, and in fact inverts, the assumption that revealing an "essential" is the most politically useful sort of act. Further, her analysis of the "homophobic phantasmatic" in *Excitable Speech*, 111, shows the potential perils of gay self-identification. This theme of strategic revealing of one's sexual identity will be taken up further in chapter 4.

28. Charles Taylor, *The Ethics of Authenticity* (Cambridge: Harvard University Press, 1991), 52. See also Hans-Georg Gadamer, *Truth and Method* (New York: Continuum, 1995), 302–307.

29. Michel Foucault, *The History of Sexuality, Vol. I* (New York: Vintage, 1978), 6.

30. Buber, *Between Man and Man*, 104.

31. Buber, *Between Man and Man*, 105.

32. Buber, *Between Man and Man*, 105.

33. Buber, *Between Man and Man*, 106–107.

34. Buber, *Between Man and Man*, 106.

35. Buber, *Between Man and Man*, 107.

36. Buber, *Between Man and Man*, 113.

37. Buber, *Between Man and Man*, 113.

38. Buber, *Between Man and Man*, 113.

39. Buber describes the I–Thou encounter like this: "The world as experience belongs to the basic word I–It. The basic word I–You establishes the world of relation. . . . The You encounters me by grace—it cannot be found by seeking. But that I speak the basic word to it is a deed of my whole being, is my essential deed.

The You encounters me. But I enter into a direct relationship to it. Thus the relationship is election and electing, passive and active at once: An action of the whole being must approach passivity, for it does away with all partial actions and thus with any sense of action, which always depends on limited exertions.

The basic word I–You can be spoken only with one's whole being. The concentration and fusion into a whole being can never be accomplished by me, can never be accomplished without me. I require a You to become; becoming I, I say You.

All actual life is encounter." Martin Buber, *I and Thou* (New York: Charles Scribner's Sons, 1970), 56, 62.

40. Nell Noddings, *Caring: A Feminine Approach to Ethics & Moral Education* (Berkeley: University of California Press, 1984), 182.

41. Noddings, *Caring*, 193.

42. Noddings, *Caring*, 179.

43. Noddings, *Caring*, 196.

44. Noddings, *Caring*, 196.

45. Buber, *Knowledge of Man*, 71.

46. Friedman, *Confirmation of Otherness*, 6.

47. This phrase comes from John Stewart, in conversation.

48. Cited in Friedman, *Confirmation of Otherness*, 28–29.

49. By saying "Hegelian" here, I mean that Hegel philosophized a historical understanding of human beings. As history progresses, so does humankind. When Taylor makes statements such as "the age of dignity was born" ("The Politics of Recognition," 49), he echoes the Hegelian sentiment that human relations transform from age to age, that history changes us, that one can identify some human forms of consciousness to be of this period and some of that period. For a discussion on Hegel, history, and consciousness, see Peter Singer, *Hegel* (New York: Oxford University Press, 1983), 9–23.

50. Buber, *Knowledge of Man*, 67.

51. Ernest J. Gaines, *A Lesson before Dying* (New York: Knopf, 1993).

52. Patricia J. Williams, *The Alchemy of Race and Rights: Diary of a Law Professor* (Cambridge: Harvard University Press, 1991), 68.

53. Gaines, *A Lesson*, 100.

54. Gaines, *A Lesson*, 100.

55. This death-row event of sheer educational presence is not unlike the existential event of terminal illness in the doctor–patient relationship that Gadamer describes in *The Enigma of Health*. Gadamer notes that when patients are diagnosed as terminally ill, *that* is when the real work of healing sets in. No longer can the doctor (or in our case the teacher) rely on technological advances (or in our case pedagogical techniques); what is left is the existential encounter itself. See Hans-Georg Gadamer, *The Enigma of Health*, translated by Jason Gaiger and Nicholas Walker (Cambridge: Polity Press, 1996).

56. Buber, *Between Man and Man*, 89.

57. Gaines, *A Lesson*, 234.

58. Brice R. Wachterhauser, ed., *Hermeneutics and Modern Philosophy* (Albany: SUNY Press, 1986), 292.

59. Cited in James Risser, *Hermeneutics and the Voice of the Other* (Albany: SUNY Press, 1997), 92.

60. Risser, *Voice of the Other*, 92.

61. By bringing in the preceding example of confirmation at our STAR group,

I realize that I have stepped into a very complicated discourse on student resistance to transformational pedagogy. This complicated discourse raises the following sorts of questions: Why did these students choose extracurricular as opposed to classroom means to act out against racism? Was something lacking in the curriculum? Did the intersection of student identities and teacher identities have anything to do with the choice of these students to join an after-school group? I do not mean to try to simplify the complexity of student resistance to classroom learning by suggesting that they needed confirmation instead of abstract learning. I can only speculate that such may have been the case for the members of our STAR group. Whether the motivation for joining the group came from a need for confirmation, or whether the motivation came from resistance to in-class measures of fostering racial recognition, is not my point.

My experience with nonclassroom forms of empowerment is not isolated. Elizabeth Ellsworth's experience at the University of Wisconsin–Madison is much the same. Ellsworth speaks to the fallibility of classroom dialogue and of pedagogies of "knowing" the other. See her "Why Doesn't This Feel Empowering?" in *Harvard Educational Review* (August 1989), 297–324.

4

On the Discursive Limits of the Encounter: Subjection

To be addressed is not merely to be recognized, but to have the very term conferred by which the recognition of existence becomes possible.

—Judith Butler[1]

Who am I when *dat* teacher already knows who I am?

—Olivia, interpreted

While I have so far taken a more in-depth look at the knowledge-gaining and affirming aspects of the encounter, I have not yet pushed the issue of the *re* of *recognition*. This *re* hints at a certain movement of repetition within the encounter. What might it mean if recognition is, in part, a re-cognition? When I re-cognize the other, what am I doing yet again? Even more pointedly, if I am doing something over when I recognize a person, then to what extent can I be recognizing that person as a unique individual? If the other seems to be conforming to a set of understandings that are already available to me, then when I recognize that person is he or she not being subjected, being forced into a pre-understood way of being?

Or, to turn these questions around: When I am recognized by an other, to what extent am I already fitting into a set of understandings that is already available to that person? What preformulated stereotypes, preformulated matrices, or rigid generalities might be dominating my uniqueness, my specific life experience? How happy can I be to be recognized if that recognition is not specific to *me*? To what extent is recognition of me a matter of subjection?

Clearly, questions of subjection like these tread on terrain distant from the recognitive concerns that we have been looking into. Recall that Taylor is concerned with recognizing the unique cultural identity of the other, and that Buber is concerned with confirming the unanticipatible existence of the other. What is apparent about these two recognitive perspectives from the subjection-referenced orientation of Judith Butler is that they take recognition to be primarily an act of individuals who are confirming while paying little attention to the invasive presence of social power when it comes to recognition.

SUBJECTION AND CULTURAL ASSUMPTIONS

Butler's conception of the encounter starts with the assumption that neither knowledge nor acknowledgment is ever just ours to decide, that recognition always takes place within a larger horizon of socially imbued discourses, and that those discourses are circumscribed by social power, institutional constraints, and hegemonic norming. Both knowing *about* a person and *confirming* a person need to be considered within the context of the largely unspoken cultural assumptions that inform them. Such cultural assumptions are all the more prevalent, and all the more enforced, in the "ideological state apparatus" of the school, to borrow Louis Althusser's term.[2] Butler's rendering of the encounter suggests that any analysis of recognition must also include skepticism about the ability of both mirroring and confirmation to be acts of positive acknowledgment pure and simple.

I begin with two illustrative scenarios from a college classroom in which a teacher is recognized by her students. These situations are different from any of those analyzed so far in that this one involves a teacher, and not a student, who is being acknowledged. Clearly, though, the encounter is a two-way street.[3] Being a teacher does not mean that one does not look for recognition. Recognition can be at play for any person who encounters another. The following scenarios are rendered from the point of view of the classroom instructor, Kate Evans. They are her own descriptions.[4]

Two Classroom Scenarios

Scenario #1: I am teaching a course at a community college where we are exploring issues of identity and contemporary controversial issues through reading a variety of texts, including poetry, memoir, newspaper articles, essays, and short fiction. While discussing and writing about issues and themes that the texts raise, the students often draw on their own experiences. I become increasingly aware of a tension I am feeling as facilitator of this group, a tension I have not felt in the past. This tension has to do with occasions in which I also want to draw on my own experiences in class discussions—and then I stop myself short of sharing any details of my life that might implicate me as a lesbian. This tension is new in that I have only recently fallen in love with a woman; most of my prior teaching life I was in a relationship with a man. I decide I want to "come out" to my students. I want to do it deliberately. And so I plan it.

I decide that a good time to come out to my students will be when they are writing and talking about times they have been discriminated against, and times in which they have harbored prejudices against others. During class, when students are talking about times they feel like outsiders, they are drawing on personal experiences, mostly examples relating to their racial or ethnic backgrounds. For instance, Enrico, a Mexican American, says he is often followed around stores in the mall by security because he "looks like a Mexican and wears baggy pants." Shawn, a black man, tells of regularly being pulled over by police in "white" neighborhoods. Vi, a woman of Vietnamese descent who was born in the U.S., says she's tired of people asking her, "Where are you from?" When I realize I am about to come out to the students, my heart begins to race and my arms to tingle. I then tell the students that I, too, sometimes feel like an outsider because "I'm gay." The class falls quiet. Everyone looks at me.

Then Nicole raises her hand and asks, "How long have you known you're gay?" I take a breath and answer. Then another student asks me a question. And another. They ask me questions for the remaining hour of class. Someone wants to know, "Why do some lesbians 'dress like men'?" Another wants to know, "What do your parents think?" Someone even asks me, "Do you think Tom Cruise is cute?" When class time is up, students clearly want to continue talking about the topic, so I tell them we can continue the next class session.

Scenario #2: I am teaching a required foundations course in a teacher education program. Our third day of class, during small group discussions, a student is talking about parental influence on children's lives. To draw me in, and perhaps to ask me to elucidate a point, he says, "You have children, right? What do you think?" At this point, I am wondering two things: *Why would he think I have children? And, am going to come out?* Even though by this time I have come out often, in a variety of ways in a variety of scenarios, once again my heart races and my palms get sweaty.

The rest of the conversation goes like this:

Me: No, I don't have children.

Student: Oh, I thought you did. But you're married, aren't you?

Me: I would be if I could be.

Student: (Pause) What do you mean?

Me: I'm not legally allowed to marry Annie, the woman I love. We've been together for three years.

Student: Oh? Oh. You're, you're in a relationship with a woman.

Me: Uh huh.

Student: And gay people can't get married? Really?

Me: Yep.

Student: Oh, but I've seen two women get married on TV. You know, like on *Friends*.

Me: Well people do it, but it's not legally binding. The person performing the ceremony has to leave out, "By the power vested in me by the state of *blank*." We haven't had a ceremony, no, if that's what you're asking.

Student: Oh really.

Subjection Theorized

Leaving these two scenarios suspended to revisit later, let us first look at Butler's conception of recognition's subjection, or rather, recognition's subject. The word *subject* is as good a place to start as any. As Butler points out, there are two connotations of the term *subject* that are problematically linked. To be a subject means both to be an autonomous figure (as in the self who is a philosophical subject) and to be subjected to an external power (as in the underling who is a king's subject). Butler writes that " 'subjection' signifies the process of becoming subordinated by power as well as the process of becoming a subject."[5] Taking this double signification of subject seriously, Butler suggests that being who I am is always also a matter of being me according to what culture has available for me to be.

To flesh out the subject/subjection problem, which is also an alternative description of the recognition/re-cognition problem, I turn to Butler's analysis of gender. As I intimated earlier, Butler revises the way sex and gender are typically understood in modern European cultures. She points out that often gender is theorized as a societal "role" that is assigned to biological males and females. As she puts it, gender is usually "conceived merely as the cultural inscription of meaning on a pre-given sex."[6] In this typical understanding of gender, the way a man acts is male, and the way a woman acts is female. Biological substance is posited as the real sex of a person, and then cultural expectations, norms, rituals, and conventions mold the raw material of biological sex into the cultural practice of being masculine or feminine. In this popular account of gender, gender is to culture as sex is to nature. Following this account, there is a pregiven subject who is either male or female. The male subject, for instance, may act in this or that masculine way, but he is fundamentally a male.

If there is any doubt that the above logic guides prevalent understandings of gender, one only need look to the recent *Diagnostic and Statistical Manual* (DSM III) for clinical psychology.[7] Within the pages of the DSM III, the recommended protocol for diagnosing "gender identity disorder" bears out this popular nature/culture logic of the sex/gender split. A child can be identified with gender identity disorder if he or she does not follow the culturally acceptable practices of his or her sex. If the child is a boy, for example, he can be diagnosed with gender identity disorder if he acts effeminate by partaking in too many cultural activities that are identified as female. The DSM III offers a clinical diagnosis protocol for boys who display a "preoccupation with female stereotypical activities as manifested by a preference for either cross-dressing or simulating female attire, or by a compelling desire to participate in the games and pastimes of girls."[8] In this typical approach to the concept of gender, there is a core conception of biology-as-sex. The boy with gender identity disorder is the one who does not properly adhere to the cultural conventions that "should" affix to his biological destiny.

But Butler points out that the logic of the sex/gender taxonomy is a formulation that obfuscates the cultural underpinnings of biological sex itself. Biological sex is in fact not "radically unconstructed," argues Butler.

> Gender is not to culture as sex is to nature; gender is also the discursive/ cultural means by which "sexed nature" or "a natural sex" is produced and established as "prediscursive," prior to culture, a politically neutral surface *on which* culture acts.[9]

That is to say, the practice of distinguishing between *feminine* (culture) and *girl* (nature) is itself what makes *girl* seem stable. The very girl-ness of a girl does not make any sense except in relation to the cultural expectations that posit femininity as a cultural skin that surrounds the biological girl. As Butler puts it, there is no "prediscursive" life of "natural" gender. The very ability to posit sex/gender as part of a nature/culture logic is itself dependent upon the societal discourses that relegate some aspects of humanity to a more natural state than others. "This production of sex *as* the prediscursive ought to be understood as the effect of the apparatus of cultural construction designated by *gender*."[10] The naturalness of sex, whatever its nature is, and the culturalness of gender, whatever its nature is, are facts that are themselves determined by the discourses surrounding the notion of gender.

Butler argues that gender should not be posited vertically, on top of sex, like a humanly constructed building on top of a "natural" ground. Rather, gender should be seen as a lateral instantiation of cultural practices "which, jointly, construct the illusion of a primary and interior gendered self."[11]

There is no core sex that waits dormant, ready to be practiced as "gender." The coreness of sex is an attribute of a certain understanding of gender. Gender, in turn, is a practice that is informed "laterally" by the practices of others over the course of history. Being gendered consists of taking up a way of being—being either "male" or "female"—that has long been understood as being gendered. It means taking up a set of cultural cues that make sense due to predetermined notions of male/female binary. It means stepping into a conversation that is already going on.

Butler's critique of the sex/gender taxonomy is a useful heuristic device for theorizing the subject/subjection problem. Following Butler's analysis of the discursive constitution of sex, the "true" subject, the subject that is assumed to be at one's core, is constituted just like the "true" man that is assumed to be at the core of "male." Just as "man" is an outcome of a discursive practice that poses "man" as the natural origin of masculinity, so too one's "core self" is the outcome of a discursive practice that poses a difference between surface practices and deep practices, between cultural scripts and essential ways of being. One's core self is inaugurated by the discursive positing of a noncore self. Another way of saying this is that the subject comes into being by means of subjection. One's core self is beholden to that which is "outside" of it. Who I am, deep down, is not about who I am as much as it is about the social scripts that allow who I am to come into being. The essential *I* is always already subjected to the discursive constitution of the nonessential *I*.

Subject-ion and Re-cognition

This double meaning of the subject has direct bearing on the encounter, and on the *re* of recognition. Following the intersubjective tenets of our discussion so far, it is through the encounter, through recognition, that the subject comes to be acknowledged. Whether it be during the public recognition that Taylor advocates, or whether it be during the I–Thou encounter described by Buber, subjectivity is shored up between self and other. In Taylor's terms, "My own identity crucially depends on my dialogical relations with others."[12] But the encounter is an instance that also inaugurates subjection insofar as it inaugurates the subject, or brings "me" into being. Following the general logic of Butler's subject/subjection problematic, the encounter takes on the more substantial role of (re)producing the subject.

My reading of Butler questions the vertical orientation of liberal recognition looked at earlier. Using Butler's lateral analysis of identity, recognition is a much more complicated process than Taylor realizes. Taylor's notion of recognition suggests that there is a core identity experienced at home "in a continuing dialogue and struggle with significant others."[13] A person then arrives at the public scene with this "authentic" identity. Taylor points out that "There is a certain way of being that is *my* way," and that I need recognition in the public sphere.[14] Thus, according to Taylor, "What has come about with the modern age is not the need for recognition but the conditions in which this can fail."[15] This liberal version suggests that one establishes subjectivity in the private sphere and then one either experiences recognition or misrecognition during the public encounter. Misrecognition, following this understanding, is something that may, unhappily, happen to the core self.

A Butlerian critique of this position is that the very "authentic" self that is supposed to be either recognized or misrecognized is in fact a *result* of the event of being recognized/misrecognized. The very notion of authenticity is born within discourses of recognition. A liberal discourse of recognition such as Taylor's creates a vertical distinction between one world (the authentic one) and another world (the inauthentic one).[16]

Regarding this discursive creation of the "authentic" self, it is instructive to look again at Charles Taylor's "historical" discussion of the advent of the modern need for recognition. As cited earlier, Taylor writes,

> What has come about with the modern age is not the need for recognition but the conditions in which this can fail. And that is why the need is now *acknowledged* for the first time. In premodern times, people didn't speak of "identity" and "recognition," not because people didn't have (what we call) identities or because these didn't depend on recognition, but rather because these were then too unproblematic to be thematized as such.[17]

One might say that this is exactly the sort of discursive constitution of core identity to which Judith Butler refers. Taylor, within his discourse on liberal recognition, is forced to posit a premodern, authentic identity that people just didn't speak of! His discourse brings about a vertical taxonomy. The bottom line here, as I see it, is that even an encounter that claims to acknowledge an authentic self is still an event of subjection. The notion of authenticity is itself a discourse that is scripted elsewhere.

In addition, tropes such as "mirroring" themselves create the vertical taxonomy that posits one's authentic self as deep, thereby distinguishing that deep self from the "reflections" offered by others. Commonsense understandings of mirroring maintain that the mirror is merely an image of some more substantive reality. Inserted into a discourse of liberal recognition, tropes of mirroring consolidate the illusion of two distinct worlds, one more "real" than the other. But the doer, as Butler argues, is brought about by the deed.[18] The self neither has an essential "horizon," as Taylor maintains it does, nor is identity vertical and taxonomic.[19] A recognitive discourse such as Taylor's brings about, just as it results from, notions of "true" identity.

For Butler, the symbiotic relation between subject and subjection is less a taxonomic matter than it is a matter of lateral referral. Butler replaces the vertical image with a horizontal one. The encounter is not a matter of figuring out how to represent or engage with an authentic self. Rather it is a matter of reiterating the discursive cues that are already available within culture at large. Butler writes,

> There is no self that is prior to the convergence [of identity discourses] or who maintains "integrity" prior to its entrance into this conflicted social field. There is only a taking up of the tools where they lie, where the very "taking up" is enabled by the tool lying there.[20]

The encounter is circumscribed, and made possible, by the tools of cultural discourse. It is imbued with the discursive scripts that make the other intelligible to the one who recognizes. Likewise, the one who is being recognized is limited in how he or she will be recognized by the discourses (whether they be liberal, existential, or otherwise) that make that quest for recognition possible in the first place. The encounter is the instantiation of a cultural conversation between self and other that has already begun before the participants arrive.

Even the very first encounter of a person's life happens in the form of joining a conversation. Think of the paradoxical situation of a child who recognizes his mother as his mother. Hans-Georg Gadamer addresses this early instance of recognition that must, at the same time, be a re-cognition. He wonders how a child can recognize, or know, his or her mother for the first time:

> when we say "to know" we mean "to recognize," that is, to pick something out of the stream of images flowing past as being identical. What is picked out in this fashion is clearly retained. But how? When does a child know its mother for the first time? When it sees her for the first time? No. Then when? How does it take place? Can we really say at all that there is a single event in which a first knowing extricates the child from the darkness of not knowing? It seems obvious to me that we cannot.[21]

During this paradoxical "event," and I put "event" in quotations here because, as Gadamer points out, it is just as much an *invent* as it is an *event*, cognition proves to be a re-cognition of a social conversation that has been "cognized" umpteen times before. A child *re*cognizes his or her mother not from some "darkness of not knowing," but because he or she has entered a language game of which "my mother" was already an available move. The *re* of *re*cognition begins even as soon as recognition is first practiced.

Subject-ion and Agency

So far, my reading of Butler has focused on a critique of versions of interhuman encounters that claim to be able to identify or confirm some authentic other. Ended there, the lateral understanding of identity seems to be fundamentally deconstructive and not of much use for educating in the sense that education ought to *lead one out* somewhere. Indeed, this is a quite widespread interpretation of poststructuralists like Butler—that they have a lot of critiques but offer no substantive suggestions for human flourishing. Charles Taylor, for example, dismisses such "subjectivist, half-baked neo-Nietzschean theories" because according to these theories "the question is no more one of respect, but of taking sides, of solidarity."[22] Butler's presentation would indeed be half-baked if it did not contain a vision of respect.

There is, however, such a vision in Butler. The strength is that her vision does not assume that respect of an authentic self is the only sort of respect possible. In fact, Butler points out that a project of authenticity can ultimately be disrespectful to those who are being authenticated. She suggests that the vertical understanding of authenticity is a pitfall that needs to be avoided, and that a lateral conception is a necessary political move. Specifically, in cases such as where a cultural, gender, or sexual identity is to be recognized (say, in Taylor's liberal sense), the very act of recognition can be at the same time an act of essentializing what it means to be of a certain culture, a certain gender, or a certain sexuality. But as Butler points out with regard to gender, one must not forget that "that very interiority is an effect and function of a decidedly public and social discourse."[23] What if the "decidedly public and social discourse" is, at present, a disadvantage to one who seeks recognition? What sort of respect is possible if being authenticated is not to one's liking? What if the sort of respect one wants does not require authenticating by an other? What if respect requires, instead, that the "authentic" version of self be challenged?

Take, for instance, the liberal recognitive practice of advocating gender recognition in the public sphere. Advocating such public recognition for women presumes a certain vision of the gendered self. Butler worries that "the displacement of a political and discursive origin of gender identity onto a psychological 'core' precludes an analysis of the political constitution of the gendered subject."[24] That is, the acknowledgment of an authentic gendered self misses the important insight that recognition creates authenticity in ways that are not politically neutral. In the case of gender, masculine domination and compulsory heterosexuality are quite instrumental in shaping what is available to be "known" about gender identities. If gender is naturalized as a core facet of self, then these discursive practices are naturalized with it. By assuming that there is an authentic gendered identity that needs to be well mirrored, one may already be beginning downstream of a political analysis of masculine domination and compulsory heterosexuality.

As I read Butler (through a lens of recognition), authenticating tendencies are also dangerous for a broader range of cultural, racial, and sexual identity positions. If, during the encounter, one aims to shore up the authentic identity of an other, one risks ossifying an identity position that may already be demeaned, or presented as deviant, in the larger social arena. If, for example, heterosexist scripts are already in use, then authenticating the other's gay identity may be tantamount to practicing heterosexism once again. Naturalizing authentication takes away from attention to the cues that make authentication possible. The public recognition of a person's authentic identity, the very statement "I recognize and appreciate that you are gay," while seeming to show respect to that person's authentic identity, may in fact be reiterating the prejudices, stereotypes, and material disadvantages that have come to be "naturally" associated with gay identity. As Butler puts it, "names have a history, one that is invoked and reconsolidated at the moment of utterance."[25]

A discursively minded event of recognition would pay less attention to the core self of the other and more attention to the discourses that are available during that encounter. Regarding the availability of discourses, Butler writes:

> The speaking subject makes his or her decision only in the context of an already circumscribed field of linguistic possibilities. One decides on the condition of an already decided field of language, but this repetition does not constitute the decision of the speaking subject as a redundancy. The gap between redundancy and repetition is the space of agency.[26]

Opportunities for recognitive agency lie within the discourses that are already available. For Butler, a discursively ameliorative encounter will turn limiting scripts back on themselves, shedding unforeseen light on the discourses that make the encounter possible. Though all one can do is repeat, that does not mean that recognition must be redundant. Contrary to critiques that projects like Butler's offer no vision for political change, Butler highlights agency as a "possibility of a variation on that repetition."[27] When repetition surprises the discursive expectations of self and other, when it carries with it promise instead of pain, then agency is possible. In Butler's words, "There is no possibility of *not* repeating. The only question that remains is: How will that repetition occur, at what site, juridical or nonjuridical, and with what pain and promise?"[28] Respect, for Butler, has more to do with the discursive negotiation of promise than with the affirmation of authenticity.

If we accept the poststructuralist insight that identity, like language itself, becomes intelligible because it repeats cultural scripts that have already been repeated in the past, then one's horizon is already circumscribed by the historical discourses that are already available. At first glance, this seems like a defeatist attitude. After all, if identity scripts are decided in advance, what hope is there to improve upon things if we cannot choose not to repeat? Butler's point is that even if we cannot choose *whether* to repeat, we can still choose *where* to repeat. We can also choose what effect such repetition may have. Thus, the "pain and promise" of how one's identity gets interpreted will depend upon strategic uses of repetition. I would add, in the spirit of this study of recognition, that such "pain and promise" is a matter for "insiders" to decide. Where, and to what effect, one engages in repetition is best decided by the person who is being recognized.

Classroom Subjection

Having unpacked Butler's notion of recognitive subjection, let us return to the classroom scenarios with which we began this chapter.[29] While the preceding analysis was cast in theoretical terms, the following one will explore a discursive theory of the encounter. These encounters were instances where the students were in a position to afford recognition to their teacher, Kate Evans. The following analysis will draw on the interpretations of these scenarios that Evans and I have made. Together, we use Butler's performative lens to theorize classroom recognition. We look to the re-cognitive implications in this quintessentially recognitive moment of a lesbian coming out to her class. We ask: How does Butler's notion of subjection inform these scenarios? Does this poststructuralist lens offer a significant vocabulary for agency in such a situation? What sort of agentive insight is possible when an encounter is conceived of not as a recognition of some core reality but as an instantiation of discursive effects?

To address these questions, we compare the agentive possibilities of the two scenarios presented at the beginning of this chapter. In the first scenario, Evans uses a liberal model of recognition to tell the "truth" about herself. In the first story, she has been feeling uncomfortable withholding details that might reveal her lesbian status; she wants to be recognized. Thus she comes out to her students deliberately because it is better for them to know the "truth," the authentic teacher. She uses a liberal recognitive conception of agency, where a description is used to mirror the authentic, where one makes use of the "speaker's benefit," in Foucault's term.[30]

Evans's analysis: *If I describe myself "truthfully," with words that fit my "core self," then students will learn to be tolerant of me and my "true" identity, and I will be more fully "there" for them. For me, the move is not easy, but it is the obvious thing to do. I tell them I am gay.[31] I confess my gayness.*

There is certainly a rich humanistic appeal to telling the "truth" about oneself, and we do not mean to say that this sort of authentic truth should not be told. Nor do we want to say that there are not many gains to be made, both in terms of distributive equity and cultural recognition, by a certain "in your face" confession based on the mirror model of recognition. Moreover, we are not advocating a foundational model of lateral analysis that would preclude the possibility of mirroring. To make the foundational claim that one framework precludes the other would be taking a God's-eye view that precludes the very discursive embeddedness upon which a lateral analysis insists. It would be to claim in advance that one discourse should be sovereign, thus naturalizing the very (lateral) discourse that one wants to use. Mirroring, for example, is a discourse that may need to be taken up if its consequences bring promise instead of pain.[32] Rather, we want to point out that a discursive theory of the encounter has consequences that are central to a nuanced conception of agency. The "gap between redundancy and repetition" that Butler points to as the space for possible agency is a space that should not be overlooked. Or, as Michel Foucault simply put it, "there are more secrets, more possible freedoms, and more inventions in our future than we can imagine in humanism."[33] Recognitive liberalism is such a humanism.

Evans's analysis: *What are the discursive implications of my disclosure in that first scenario? What else—other than telling the whole "truth"—am I left to do in this first scenario? What happens when I turn this into a "teachable moment"? What happens when I answer my students' questions, the questions that ask, "So, what is it like to be gay-you?"*

Through the lens of our lateral analysis, there I sit, reified, concretized, making myself more and more intelligible within the homosexual/heterosexual binary as I attempt to answer each question. And because I am responding informed by the representational discourse of clarity, of intelligibility, it is as though I am working toward making "gay" safe and stable, not provocative in any way. I answer their questions head-on, though I am not sure now where these answers lead other than to promote students' tolerance of a teacher whom they really liked even before I came out! How to step outside of the individualizing, ahistorically-posed questions about "women who dress like men" and the "cuteness of Tom Cruise"? How to contest the particular configurations of gayness that already come to mind as soon as the word "gay" is spoken? What visions of being gay do the students already have in mind when the first question is asked, a question that frames gayness as essence: "How long have you known you were gay?"

A discursive analysis reminds us of the presuppositions that make intelligibility possible in the first place. The enactment of this first coming-out scenario makes "gay me" both opaque and transparent, as when a pinwheel is spinning so fast it is not seen. What is seen is "me." What is not seen, but is definitely present within the spinning, are all of the others who have confessed within the homosexual/heterosexual binary, those who have been compelled to reveal the "truth." Through the confessional act, the coming out, the "real" is surfaced. The enactment of "I'm gay" repeats and conceals the ways in which recognition is "both conditioned and circumscribed by historical convention."[34] Following Butler's lateral assessment, Evans's words are bringing about what the history of coming out as gay says she is. This is the discourse that she picks up and enacts, the discourse of revealing the authentic "truth" about herself.

Evans's analysis: *It is as though that whole semester I'd been chasing myself around the room, and then I caught up with myself, with the "truth" of my identity, and declared, "Tag, you're it. Fag, you're it."*

The first scenario is a recognitive moment in which the stigma ended up accompanying the declaration. Through the lateral lens that Butler offers, it is an example of a less-than-agentive discursive moment, for it tends to reproduce, rather than to rearticulate, regulatory norms.[35]

In contrast to that first "I'm gay," the second scenario entails an agentive gesture that is theoretically informed by the discursive gap that Butler describes. Certainly the second story has limitations as well, but we believe that scenario illustrates the way that a discursive analysis provides a significant vocabulary for agency. Recall that in the second story, Evans is asked if she is married. There are at least three ways she could have answered.

Evans's analysis: *I could have answered, "No." This response, given in the midst of the recognitive encounter, would have been informed by the logic of mirroring as was the response in the first scenario. This response would have been subject to the discursive norms as was the confessional response of "truth" in that first scenario. In particular, such a response re-inscribes people as always already heterosexual. A simple "no" makes me straight because marriage always has to do with being straight. This insight into the implications of such a mirroring response is afforded by a discursive sensibility on recognition.*

I also could have answered, "No, I'm gay." From a mirroring perspective of a discourse on the authentic self, this response enacts gayness and thus entails the same potentialities as did the first scenario as far as the humanist project of subjects who are fully "present" to one another is concerned. Similarly, this confession opens onto a discursive field that is potentially reifying, subject to the vicis-

situdes of discourse, as we noted with regard to the first scenario. However, if this response had been given, it would have entailed another facet that goes unnoticed by a mirroring view: Such an answer leaves unproblematized the fact that gays cannot legally marry.[36] *Quite simply, a lateral analysis urges us to foreground the discursive web surrounding speech, reminding us that such a web is inextricably linked to the enunciation. In this case, marriage cannot be extricated from a web of heteronormativity.*

A third response to "Are you married?" is the one I used in the story: "I would be if I could be." Seen through a discursive lens, this enactment of "gayness" works toward "the possibility for the speech act to take on non-ordinary meaning . . . one that offers an unanticipated political future for deconstructive thinking."[37] *"I would be if I could be" employs a recognitive challenge to heteronormativity that is sensitive to the discourses that surround gayness and marriage. It highlights the inequity of being gay instead of settling for the normalizing project of making gayness intelligible. The response "I would be if I could be" allows for a more flexible deployment of discourses that are not locked within a strictly normalizing, individualizing, descriptive framework. I can pick up or leave "gay" when the student offers it to me, as when he says, "Can't gay people get married?" Accepting the term is optional, but it is strategically useful in this case. I do so within the specificity of his question, and within the movement of the political. Highlighting the discursive inequities of "gayness," I elbow aside the heteronormativity of his question. This specific strategy for coming out opens up, as Butler puts it, "the possibility of a different sort of repeating" within the "stylized repetition of acts through time" that constitute the self.*[38]

Importantly, one can't be sure in advance that a discursive strategy will be agentive. By agentive we mean a strategy of recognition, chosen by the one-recognized, that capitalizes on the venue and the effectiveness of the repetitive act of recognition. It may very well be that one will end up on one side or the other of the gap between "redundancy" and "repetition." One can't know ahead of time whether the reaction of the interlocutor will serve to make redundant precisely the provocative discourse that one hopes to resignify. For example, a listener might dismiss the statement "I would be if I could be," letting it settle in within the discourse of the "complaining liberal." One could also imagine a listener who is unmoved by "I would if I could," a listener who is so entrenched in the "naturalness" of heterosexual marriage, in its "repetition" as a straight activity, that "I would if I could" is simply a statement of fact that elbows aside nothing.

These are quite real possibilities, yet these possibilities are themselves conceived from a lateral perspective, from the perspective that who one is, who one becomes, is always subject to the vicissitudes of language. A vocabulary of discursive recognition will necessarily include words like "failure" and "missed opportunity," just as every earthly vocabulary does. While Evans's experience (and our discursive assessment of it) was that this particular response was an agentive destabilization of the discursive assumptions of marriage, a re-inscription of that response would not have been a failure of a lateral strategy per se.

In concert with the more general agentive possibilities that are emphasized by a lateral conception of recognition, it is appropriate now to say how this lateral conception has informed my own thinking, how this particularly situated author has been, and needs to be, recognized within a discursive understanding of the encounter. While I spoke earlier to my daughter's experience at Kidsmusic, and to my experience as a teacher in South Africa and my subsequent reading in philosophy and social theory, I would like to stress now how Butler's discursive notion of recognition has foisted upon me an important dose of self-recognition regarding my position as heterosexual teacher.

What Butler has taught me is an obvious yet important lesson, one that I take to the university and high school classrooms where I currently teach, one that is discounted at the risk of partaking in oppression of others. As Butler points out, there is no personal act of recognition that is not already steeped in the sorts of recognitions that are allowed or disallowed in culture at large. Thus, when, as a heterosexual teacher, I talk about issues of heterosexuality in the classroom, when I listen to students talk about going out on dates, when I mention my female partner and my daughter, and when I congratulate students on marriages, engagements, or new children, if I engage in these sorts of recognitive practices without advocating recognition of gay, lesbian, and bisexual identity in the same public space, then the discursive effect of my actions is that of an oppressive misrecognition. In today's highly heterosexist culture, it is not a value-neutral stand for a heterosexual to recognize the heterosexual identity of another. Just being a heterosexual-who-recognizes is already implicated in the heterosexist denigration of homosexuality. To combat this, it is imperative that I "come out" as one who affirms queer identity in the classroom. Coming out is not just Kate's issue; it is mine as well.

Butler reminds me of the connection between my own act of recognizing others and the particular identity that I represent when I do that recognizing. Within the context of classroom teaching this is especially significant, since curriculum and pedagogy are too often thought of as somehow distinct from the identity of the one who does the teaching. In fact, the identity of the one-teaching, which may well coincide with the identity of the one-recognizing, is part and parcel of the recognition that curriculum and pedagogy aim to foster. When I decide what to teach, I must also decide how to use my identity to foster not only the letter but the spirit of my curriculum as well.

RECOGNITION AND CURRICULAR INTERPRETATION

My consideration of these two scenarios points to a distinctly interpretive quality of the encounter. By interpretive I mean that one has to know how to *read* the situation.

Discursive recognition depends upon the sorts of interpretive opportunities that are available within the discourses that are used at the very moment of the encounter.[39] One cannot take a God's-eye view from nowhere and decide beforehand how to recognize an other in a positive way. The very possibility of discursive recognition depends upon an interpretation using the discursive tools at hand at the particular moment of the encounter. Disruptive possibilities lie in whatever crops up to be disrupted; ameliorative possibilities depend upon the discourses that can be rearticulated in the moment.

This sort of on-the-spot interpretation is much like the confirmative coming-to-know that I pointed to earlier with relation to Gaines's text, the difference being a matter of emphasis. Butler is concerned mainly with the discursive "read" and not with the human confirmation. Butler has more to say about the discursive effects of curriculum than about the actual act of recognizing the other, I to I, or the preplanned project of recognition by means of curricular infusion. From a mirroring perspective, this interpretive quality might seem reprehensible. If the self is authentic, then it should be the same beforehand and afterwards. One need only look beforehand to a core identity to see how that core identity needs to be mirrored in the future. But, from a lateral perspective, the interpretation of which one avails oneself during the encounter is the ethical field upon which agentive possibilities arise.[40]

With this interpretive, hermeneutic quality of the encounter in mind, I want to revisit the link between curriculum and identity.[41] For while our conversation has touched on the recognitive impetus behind multicul-

tural curriculum changes, it has not yet addressed how curricular innova-
tion is interpreted, how it is read, and how such a reading gets played out
during the encounter. Curriculum is understood differently according to
the two models of recognition previously encountered in this text—
mirroring and confirmation. Taylor's mirror recognition relies upon an
understanding of curriculum-as-representation. For Taylor curriculum is
a means for the positive images of people, cultures, groups, and identities
to be represented, to shine through. Taylor believes that people look to
curriculum for positive pictures of their cultural affiliations, and his
model assumes that individuals have authentic selves that need to be mirrored in terms of their cultural affiliations. As he puts it, "There is a certain way of being human that is *my way*."[42] For Taylor, this "my way"
can depend upon cultural affiliation. The authentic, cultural self can be
represented clearly and positively by way of curriculum. According to
Taylor, we must capitalize on the representational opportunities that curriculum affords us for student recognition. Students of all walks of life
must be represented in curricula so that they are not given, "either directly or by omission, a demeaning picture of themselves."[43]

I want to point out also how far an interpretive link between identity
and curriculum is from a confirmative project of unknowability. Although we have not yet explored a direct link between Buber and curriculum, it is safe to say, given Buber's insistence on the unqualified "Yes,"
that Buber would be leery of such a curricular account of recognition.
Representational models of recognition lead toward categorization and
away from the presence of confirmation. Such presence cannot take place
through the vicarious means of curricular representation. Following
Buber, it would not be possible to front-load recognition into educational
practices by means of representational curriculum.

Indeed, this inability to place curriculum within the context of the I–
Thou relationship has caused some commentators to wonder whether
there is anything at all educationally reproducible in Buber's project. As
Adir Cohen notes, "A pedagogical model, designed to be imitated, cannot
be based on Buber's philosophy."[44] Buber's confirmation adds little to a
discourse on curriculum, though it does serve as a healthy reminder that
representation is limited in its ability to affirm human complexities.

In contrast to Buber's and Taylor's models, Butler's lateral understanding of the encounter yields a different understanding of curriculum. If
recognition is discursively constituted, then it is certainly not possible for
educators to escape or ignore representational categories as a confirma-

tive project might. Representations are already discursively in play; they cannot be bracketed. Moreover, one cannot be sure beforehand that any given piece of representation will foster positive acknowledgment. Acknowledgment will depend in part upon the immediate social cues that make a curriculum interpretable in this way or that. Even if the curriculum is front-loaded with positive images, those positive images may or may not foster positive recognition. To claim that a positive curricular picture can be made up before the actual performative enactment of recognition is to ignore the historical and cultural conventions that accompany the recognitive event. For Butler's lateral understanding of recognition, both curricular amnesia and prearranged curricular flattery are out of the question. Informed by a discursive understanding of recognition, a student's (or teacher's) reading takes place at the intersection of how such reading effects (and affects) his or her self-image, what people expect of him or her regardless of what I read, and what opportunities are acquired as a result of that reading. Positive acknowledgment of self cannot be extricated from this highly charged intersection.

Speaking to this highly charged intersection of individual circumstance and larger social cues, Butler writes,

> If the performative [and here we might substitute "the discursive encounter"] must compel collective recognition in order to work, must it compel only those kinds of recognition that are *already* institutionalized, or can it also compel a critical perspective on existing institutions? What is the performative [the discursive] power of claiming an entitlement to those terms— "justice," "democracy"—that have been articulated to exclude the ones who now claim that entitlement?[45]

Thinking specifically about educational entitlements, we might ask what effects well-meaning, well-mirroring curricula can have when injustice and un-democracy are already at work?[46] For example, what sort of recognition can a curriculum afford if hate speech runs rampant in a school? If "faggot" is the slur of choice on school grounds, what hope, or what promise, is there for the uptake of positive curricular representations of gays and lesbians? Or, what sort of promise is there for multicultural literature to promote recognition if school tracking provides de facto "evidence" of racial inequality? With these sorts of un-democracies already at work, what promise is there that curriculum will not be, in Butler's terms, merely redundant?

Ostensibly ameliorative curricular change can in fact enact misrecognition if it closes its eyes to, or winks at, wider social cues. Misrecognition can be an effect of a lack of critical interpretive exchange. This is summed up in a cynical though accurate statement made by Abdul JanMohamed and David Lloyd:

> Such pluralism [I would say such multicultural representation that is not interpretive] tolerates the existence of salsa, it even enjoys Mexican restaurants, but it bans Spanish as a medium of instruction in American schools.[47]

The duplicity that is highlighted in this cynical statement would not be a surprise for Butler. Ameliorative images must be interrogated and interpreted with an eye toward their pragmatic results. One should question not just what readings are like, but what happens as a result of readings.

Does Butler's discursive conception of recognition offer a curricular vision of recognition that is more than cynical? Yes. For Butler, it is the potential for "resignification" that makes representation ripe for agentive identification. "I would argue," writes Butler, "that it is precisely the *expropriability* of the dominant, 'authorized' discourse that constitutes one potential site of its subversive resignification."[48] It is not the content of curriculum that is paramount; it is rather the way that such content is reappropriated. For example, whether lesbians are well represented in the curriculum is important, but it is only part of the issue for a project of discursive recognition. Discursive recognition also depends upon how such representations can be reappropriated on behalf of lesbians. Ultimately, an insistence on curricular interpretation is hyperrecognitive. By this I mean that the very decision as to whether a curriculum includes, in Taylor's words, "a confining, or demeaning, or contemptible picture" is a pragmatic matter that needs to be gauged within the context of a struggle for recognition. Reappropriation of curriculum, like Kate Evans's "I would be if I could be," is as central to curricular change as what is textually represented.

For an example of how Butler's notion of discursive recognition might help educators construe curriculum differently, I examine a specific historical instance that has been recounted in many school textbooks: the story of Rosa Parks and the Montgomery bus boycott. This example has been taken up by multicultural educators and educational activists such as James Banks and Herbert Kohl.[49] Banks, for example, has pointed out how curricular representations have not done justice to this historical incident. For an understanding of this event, I will follow Banks in his critique of popular textbook accounts. Then, I will show how Butler's lateral project pushes that critique along.

Banks reviews the story of Rosa Parks and the Montgomery bus boycott of 1955 and how it is usually explained to schoolchildren. He observes that there is a disempowering discourse in schools surrounding this piece of history. To begin with, Parks is usually pictured as a tired old lady who was just fed up with having to sit in the back of the bus. On the contrary, as Parks herself notes,

> People always say that I didn't give up my seat because I was tired, but that wasn't true. I was not tired physically, or no more tired than I usually was at the end of a working day. I was not old, although some people have an image of me being old then. I was forty-two. No, the only tired I was, was tired of giving in.[50]

Such a picture has a number of errors and deceptions, though it may be attractive in its human appeal. Parks was not a lonely hero who was old and frustrated. She was part of a rich civil rights network. The Women's Political Council, founded in 1946, orchestrated the Montgomery bus boycott. Banks points out that an individualizing of the boycott, an account that ignores the broader social movement, is irresponsible if not disempowering.

Banks suggests that unveiling other interpretations of the past, especially in textbook examples such as the misleading story of Parks, is integral to creating a transformative multicultural curriculum. Educators must use transformative knowledge, such as a revision of the Parks story that highlights the Women's Political Council, to teach students "how to construct their own interpretations of the past and present."[51] As Banks explains, we must teach students "how written history can be highly discrepant from actual past events" and "how history is rewritten when people who have been excluded from its production begin to play active roles in its construction."[52] Curriculum needs to be reinterpreted from the perspective of marginalized groups. For Banks, students who are able to practice multicultural knowledge construction, especially students who have been excluded in the past from such construction, will be able to "develop a sense of personal and civic efficacy."[53] I take this to mean that students will experience cultural agency through recognition that is fostered by a transformative curriculum. That is to say, students will become empowered when they learn that they can themselves revise mirrors that are tarnished.

A discursive understanding of recognition can supplement the thinking of Banks here. In part, Banks's aim of revamping disempowering curriculum is quite in line with a critical discursive project. That is to say, both are suspicious of curricular representations, such as popular textbook accounts of Rosa Parks, which pretend to be clear windows onto reality. Just as in Butler's account of gender identity, Banks highlights the cultural cues that go hand-in-hand with what we perceive to be authentic. Just as a girl is just a "girl" until one challenges the cultural cues that actually bring girlhood into being, Rosa Parks is just "tired old Rosa Parks" until one challenges the psychologizing cultural cues that surround that particular presentation of Parks. If a student looks for mirroring in the popular textbook account of "tired old Rosa Parks," then he or she will attain representational recognition that is subject to all of the psychologizing discursive cues that have a bearing on that popular account. Mirroring has social, as well as personal, meaning.

Butler's conception of performative recognition suggests a healthy skepticism that is an important augmentation of Banks's project. Butler reminds us that recognition is not only a matter of mirrors, but it is also a matter of classroom interpretation. Not only must curriculum be transformed, but it must be read differently, and acted upon with results, by students. Educators must also pay attention to the immediate cultural cues that attend mirroring within the public space of the classroom. Whether personal and social agency can be attained cannot be decided beforehand by looking only to the degree to which content is transformative. How transformative content gets interpreted and acted upon is just as important as the initial transforming of the content. Significantly, for the purposes of this study of the encounter, content gets interpreted and acted upon during the intersubjective circumstances of self–other recognition.

A discursive understanding of curriculum is thus not a critique of transformative knowledge per se. On the contrary, a performative scrutiny of the event of recognition suggests that even more weight be accorded to the transformative quality of knowledge. With the help of Butler, we can identify more precisely the requirement that knowledge must indeed transform if it is to be useful. If the event of recognition is not itself transformative, then the transformative quality of knowledge will be lost. If texts are not interpreted in agentive ways, if they are not read in ways that promote social and personal change, then the texts are not transformative after all.

In fact, Butler's warning that recognition depends upon the event, upon the uptake, suggests something in addition to the fact that transformative knowledge must be put into play carefully, with an eye toward interpretation. Her warning also urges that even hegemonic knowledge might suffice as a critical mirror for recognition if the event of recognition is appropriately expropriate. That is to say, returning to Butler's insistence that the "expropriation" of dominant discourses "constitutes one potential site of its subversive resignification," we can note that even typical curricular images such as "tired old Rosa Parks" might be reclaimed as sources of positive recognition.

This resignification of dominant discourses is where Butler's pragmatic, discursive account of recognition strays most significantly from the revised Parks story that Banks and Kohl offer. Neither Banks nor Kohl tenders the possibility that reclaiming the Parks stereotypical history might be just as empowering as knowing the "truth" about the Women's Political Council. Butler's question is, Which is more important, "truth" or agency? Her answer is the latter. This scrutiny of "truth" vis-à-vis agency is reminiscent of Evans's decision to use marriage as the focus of a coming-out strategy. She uses marriage as a politically calculating strategy even though the "truth" about marriage is that it is a quintessential heterosexist practice. During the event of her own recognition, she feels less obliged to get at all levels of the "truth" than to make the event into an empowering moment.

In short, recognition depends on the transformative quality of the interpretive uptake just as much as it does on the transformative quality of curricular content. Many more texts may be ripe for recognitive resignification than those that are deemed "transformative" by educators who construct such curricula. For example, "tired old Rosa" might turn out to be an agentive concept, an agentive slogan, within the encounter. Transformative potential depends upon the encounter between selves, texts, and others.

THE LIMITS AND OPPORTUNITIES OF DISCURSIVITY AND EDUCATION

It is imperative to note the limitations of Butler's discursive theorizing. These limitations are quite concrete, in the literal sense of the word, as

Butler constantly deprioritizes the physical surroundings that inevitably constrain or empower human beings who come together to recognize and be recognized.

Consider, for instance, the historic imagery of the public forum evoked by Taylor's story of how recognition has come to play an integral part in the modern politics of human dignity. Or consider the passage cited earlier from Buber's description of the human being, in need of confirmation, who "watches for a Yes which allows him to be and which can only come to him from one human person to another."[54] In these examples, there is a highlighting of the physical situation that clears a space for human presence.

In contrast, Butler's discursive theorizing of recognition does not take the sort of realist approach that might lend itself to interrogating how people are physically constrained or empowered to recognize others. Both the strength and the weakness of Butler's poststructuralist rendition of subjection is that it excavates the linguisticality of recognizing insofar as language contains the original enigma that it is already spoken before one arrives on the scene. Her analysis does not delve into the ways in which people are allowed or disallowed to choose *when* they speak and *what* they say. Thus, while Butler offers an important perspective on the ways in which discursive power preconstrains the sorts of recognition that might survive the "uptake" in any given situation, her analysis does not speak to the ways in which the institutionalization of teachers and students in schools may preclude the lived opportunity for practicing recognition.

Physical circumstances, such as school schedules that require each teacher to interact with 150 students or more per day; teacher preparation sequences that insist on "professionalism" to the exclusion of the interpersonal interest that is needed for recognition to take place; school protocols of surveillance and metal detection that foster inhuman relations between students and school officials; uses of technology that preclude intersubjective presence; authoritarian relationships between teachers and students that are fostered by expectations that teachers should maintain control; teacher burn-out caused by unreasonable teaching loads—all of these are physical circumstances that are outside the scope of Butler's discursive analysis. About these concrete issues, a more extended political analysis of how recognition might be effected in the public space of the school would necessarily concern itself.

Once again, though, I want to come back to the strategy of perspectivism. These limitations to Butler's theorizing of subjection are not cause to reject her recognitive project. Butler is working within a poststructuralist discourse that does not speak to the concrete, but rather to the symbolic of human interaction. Her perspective is of great value insofar as it allows us to shift registers, to look through a different lens onto recognitive encounters.

Having noticed the more tangible educational circumstances to which a lateral perspective does not speak, I now want to offer a view of how a discursive view does indeed point to the appropriateness of the school as a site of self-formation, notwithstanding educational institutionalization and teacher circumstances. The school is an appropriate site to work on recognition-as-subjection both because schools are indeed highly contested sites where power and discourse are brought to bear on teachers and students in the space of an "ideological state apparatus," and because schools offer a uniquely situated opportunity to work against the negative effects of subjection.

Schools are places where recognition-as-subjection is ignored at our own peril. Schools, like incarceration and military institutions, are places where discursive norms are invested in people.[55] They are places where the *re* of *re*cognition is often predefined by institutional expectations, and by outright silencing. Teachers and students are the sites of such investments in obvious and insidious ways. For example, the K–12 classroom, in contradistinction to a progressive junior college such as the one analyzed earlier, has been called "the last closet."[56] Teachers are still being fired for coming out. Heterosexuality is strictly enforced in K–12 classrooms in ways that make both the teacher and the student active purveyors, if by no other means than the nonrecognition of homosexual identity in the classroom, of heterosexism. While teachers are subjected to state-mandated curriculum guidelines, scripted lesson plans, exhaustingly dehumanizing schedules of teaching 150 students per day, students are already being recognized in ways that are oppressive. Recognition takes place in schools whether or not one has taken the intersubjective time to practice affirming an other. Given the *already* of recognition, especially in an ideologically saturated space like the school, it is incumbent upon educators to combat oppressive social scripts by practicing recognition, at least to the extent that institutional constraints can be pushed to allow such positive affirmation.

A lateral conception of recognition moreover recommends the school as a place to pursue recognition by virtue of its cultural status as a literate place, because what characterizes a discursive pursuit of the encounter is its vigilance, its noninnocence. Since recognition takes place primarily within a web of historical and cultural circumstances, it cannot be primarily a matter of individuals who decide, in a facile manner, that they will acknowledge one another in a positive manner.[57] Recognition is a matter of interpreting the practical consequences of a particular encounter. In this discursive spirit of skepticism, interpretation, and the self–other encounter, recognition is most emphatically the business of those who would be educated. It is the business of those who want to be led out of dominant, unquestioned ways of being, prevailing ways of thinking, and into spaces that are opened up through inquiry and engagement. The school is an important venue for the encounter not only because it is a public space where humans seek to be authenticated, but also because recognition is a practice in reading the discursive cues in which the encounter is embedded. The encounter, as is the case with reading, is best facilitated in literate places like schools. The school as a place of meeting and intersubjective experience, a place where the encounter can be a reciprocal interaction between self and other, is central to the next chapter.

NOTES

1. Judith Butler, *Excitable Speech: A Politics of the Performative* (New York: Routledge, 1997), 5.

2. Louis Althusser, "Ideology and Ideological State Apparatuses (Notes toward an Investigation)" in *Mapping Ideology*, edited by Slavoj Zizek (New York: Verso, 1994).

3. This two-way-ness of the encounter will be the subject of the next chapter.

4. I am using Evans's own descriptions, as opposed to telling her story myself, because her rendering evokes the nuances of these recognitive encounters better than my own telling could. She and I have discussed these particular scenarios in depth, and we have both written about them elsewhere. Charles Bingham and Kate Evans, "Tag You're It, Fag You're It," presented at the Journal of Curriculum Theorizing Conference, Lexington, Kentucky, October 22, 1998. See also Kate Evans, "Are You Married?" *Multicultural Education*, forthcoming.

5. Judith Butler, *The Psychic Life of Power: Theories in Subjection* (Stanford, Calif.: Stanford University Press, 1997), 2.

6. Judith Butler, *Gender Trouble* (New York: Routledge, 1990), 7.

7. I became aware of this particular example of the sex/gender split while reading Eve Kosofsky Sedgwick's insightful analysis of the DSM III in "How to

Bring Your Kids Up Gay," *Social-Text*, 1991, 9:4(29), 18–27. See the *Diagnostic and Statistical Manual of Mental Disorders: DSM-III-R* discussion on gender identity disorder (Washington, D.C.: American Psychiatric Association, 1987).

8. Butler, *Gender Trouble*, 20.

9. Butler, *Gender Trouble*, 7.

10. Butler, *Gender Trouble*, 7. Here, I want to acknowledge a materialist critique that would challenge Butler's discursive understanding of "sex" as being too radical, as ousting biology itself. But I would say that she is not arguing that biology itself is always not-useful. It is specifically in gender and sexuality analyses that biological notions are limiting and need to be acknowledged as being discursively posited.

11. Butler, *Gender Trouble*, 138.

12. Charles Taylor, *The Ethics of Authenticity* (Cambridge: Harvard University Press, 1991), 48.

13. Charles Taylor, "The Politics of Recognition," in *Multiculturalism: Examining the Politics of Recognition*, edited by Amy Gutman (Princeton, N.J.: Princeton University Press), 37.

14. Taylor, *The Ethics of Authenticity*, 28–29.

15. Taylor, *The Ethics of Authenticity*, 48.

16. Here I am borrowing the two-world distinction that John Stewart has applied to representational language. See John Stewart, *Language as Articulate Contact* (New York: SUNY Press, 1995), 103.

17. Taylor, "The Politics of Recognition," 48.

18. See Butler's discussion of Nietzsche and the doer being brought about by the deed in *Excitable Speech*.

19. Taylor, *The Ethics of Authenticity*, 37.

20. Butler, *Gender Trouble*, 145.

21. Hans-Georg Gadamer, *Philosophical Hermeneutics*, translated by David E. Linge (Berkeley: University of California Press, 1976), 14.

22. Taylor, "The Politics of Recognition," 70. For another recent critique of Butler, see Martha Nussbaum's article in *The New Republic*, Feb. 12, 1999.

23. Butler, *Gender Trouble*, 136.

24. Butler, *Gender Trouble*, 136.

25. Butler, *Excitable Speech*, 36.

26. Butler, *Excitable Speech*, 129.

27. Butler, *Excitable Speech*, 125; Butler, *Gender Trouble*, 145.

28. Butler, *Excitable Speech*, 102.

29. The remainder of Evans's and my analysis will continue to follow the text of "Tag You're It, Fag You're It."

30. Michel Foucault, *History of Sexuality, Vol. I* (New York: Vintage, 1978), 6.

31. Our use of the word "gay" throughout this paper is not meant to suggest that we believe this is the best term to use, nor is it meant to suggest that we

would not wish to challenge the use of that term to the exclusion of "lesbian," "queer," "dyke," or "fag." The choice of using the term "gay" for the purposes of this paper is a conscious decision on our part, mainly because "gay" is the term that the teacher and the student use in the two opening stories, so that using that same term allows us to highlight actual speech encountered and used.

32. Here, I am referring back to Butler's statement that "there is no possibility of *not* repeating. The only question that remains is: How will that repetition occur, at what site, juridical or nonjuridical, and with what pain and promise?" For whom is the promise significant? Following the relation between social action and recognition that I outlined in chapter 1, I mean the promise to be significant for those who feel an affront to their dignity and for those who, together, take social action to ameliorate the circumstances that led to such an affront.

33. Michel Foucault, *Technologies of the Self: A Seminar with Michel Foucault* (Amherst: University of Massachusetts Press, 1988), 15.

34. Judith Butler, "Performative Acts and Gender Constitution: An Essay in Phenomenology and Feminist Theory," in *Writing on the Body: Female Embodiment and Feminist Theory*, edited by K. Conby et al. (New York: Columbia University Press, 1998), 404.

35. Evans has actually presented that community college coming-out experience as an agentive instance in other writings. As we have mentioned, the representational model of "truth" telling has merit. However, through the lens of the discursive limits of recognition, we are better able to capture some of its limitations. The stable gay "it" produced in that moment requires her to be the benign representative of all others who are "it." See Evans, "Are You Married?"

36. Perhaps another response, one that casts doubt on whether marriage is really the best option in our heteronormative society, would be: "I have no desire to be married, but I couldn't be even if I wanted to be."

37. Butler, *Excitable Speech*, 161.

38. Butler, "Performative Acts," 402.

39. Frank Pignatelli speaks of the reactivity of Foucault's politics in a vein similar to the sort of performativity I have in mind. See Pignatelli, "What Can I Do? Foucault on Freedom and the Question of Teacher Agency," *Educational Theory* 43 (1993): 424–425. Whereas Pignatelli focuses on reactivity in relation to equity and school procedures, I am focusing on reactivity in relation to the self in the midst of an encounter.

40. For a description of the spontaneity entailed in a pedagogy informed by performativity, see Elizabeth Ellsworth's *Teaching Positions*, especially 142, 159.

41. Among the many variations of hermeneutics, I have in mind here Hans-Georg Gadamer's primarily. As I read Judith Butler, her understanding of identity and discourse has many resonances with philosophical hermeneutics, especially with the central concern of "historically effected consciousness" that is best articulated in Gadamer's *Truth and Method*. I am thankful especially to Mikkel Borsch-

Jacobsen for his explication of this concept. My reading of Gadamer is also indebted to discussions with Deborah Kerdeman and John Stewart.

42. Taylor, *The Ethics of Authenticity*, 28.

43. Taylor, "The Politics of Recognition," 65.

44. Adir Cohen, *The Educational Philosophy of Martin Buber* (East Brunswick, N.J.: Associated University Presses, 1983), 52.

45. Butler, *Excitable Speech*, 158.

46. This term "un-democracies" derives from a lecture given by Donna Kerr at the University of Washington entitled "Why John Dewey Can't Talk with Toni Morrison," January 8, 1999. Kerr spoke of "un-democracies" such as racism, sexism, and homophobia.

47. Quoted in Cameron McCarthy, "After the Canon," 300. Abdul JanMohamed and David Lloyd, "Introduction: Minority Discourse—What Is to Be Done?" *Cultural Critique* 6, 5–17.

48. Butler, *Excitable Speech*, 157.

49. See James Banks, ed., "Transformative Knowledge, Curriculum Reform, and Action" in *Multicultural Education, Transformative Knowledge and Action: Historical and Contemporary Perspectives* (New York: Teachers College Press, 1996), 335–348. Herbert Kohl also addresses the ill presentation of the Montgomery bus boycott in his essay, "The Story of Rosa Parks and the Montgomery Bus Boycott Revisited" in Kohl, *Should We Burn Babar? Essays on Children's Literature and the Power of Stories* (New York: New Press, 1995), 30–56.

50. Banks, "Transformative Knowledge," 341.

51. Banks, "Transformative Knowledge," 344.

52. Banks, "Transformative Knowledge," 343.

53. Banks, "Transformative Knowledge," 344.

54. Martin Buber, *Knowledge of Man* (London: George Allen & Unwin, 1965), 71.

55. See Michel Foucault, *Discipline and Punish* (New York: Vintage, 1977).

56. I am borrowing this term from Rita M. Kissen, *The Last Closet: The Real Lives of Lesbian and Gay Teachers* (Portsmouth, N.H.: Heinemann, 1996).

57. I am reminded here of facile slogans that are bandied about, such as "Celebrate Diversity." Butler articulates, in a very provocative fashion, my own intuitive sense that such facile slogans are not educative where recognition is concerned.

5

Recognizing as Being Recognized: Reciprocity

At the foundation of Hegelian dialectic there is an absolute reciprocity which must be emphasized. . . . If I close the circuit, if I prevent the accomplishment of movement in two directions, I keep the other within himself.

—Franz Fanon[1]

How do I recognize *dat* teacher, the one who is recognizing me?

—Olivia, interpreted

"According to the notion of recognition," writes Hegel, self-consciousness "is possible only when each is for the other what the other is for it."[2] So far, I have not given educational consideration to this reciprocal aspect of recognition. Following Hegel's intimation here, it seems that reciprocity is an important part of the encounter with the other. Just as there are at least two people involved in the self–other encounter, so is it important that each of them takes a significant role. The one-recognized needs to have an agentive role in the encounter as well as a passive one. There needs to be a balanced relationship with the other if he or she is to flourish. Hegel illustrates this need for reciprocity when he describes the relationship of a Master to a Slave in his *Phenomenology of Spirit*.[3] Such a relationship of dominance and submission is born out of an imbalance, out of nonreciprocity. An imbalance in the recognitive encounter can lead to indignity.

In this chapter, I take up this matter of reciprocity within the pedagogical encounter. How can recognitive reciprocity be described in the classroom? What new light does the give-and-take of reciprocity shed on the

117

role of the one-recognizing? On the role of the one-recognized? Can reciprocity change the quality of the recognitive encounter? Does reciprocal recognition promote the flourishing of self and other in ways that one-way recognition does not? Is the school a place where reciprocity can be practiced among students and teachers? What changes would be needed in schools in order to make them more conducive to reciprocal recognition? These are some of the questions I will be addressing with regard to reciprocity.

The first three descriptions of the encounter looked at in this work pay attention to reciprocity in varying degrees. In Charles Taylor's work on the politics of recognition, for example, while a recognitive account of the public/private split does go a considerable way toward insisting on a public space of mirroring for individuals of nonhegemonic identity positions, the same account pays little attention to those who do the mirroring. Whether it be teachers who insist on curricular representations that mirror heretofore underrepresented individuals, or whether it be legislators who enact laws for francophone autonomy, Taylor does little to interrogate the perspective of the one-recognizing.[4] In these cases, how might a person in a position of power need to be recognized as such? I think there are serious omissions going on if the position of the one-recognizing is not made explicit, or, to put this another way, if the one-recognizing is not himself or herself recognized.

In Buber's work on confirmation, there is attention to give-and-take within the encounter. Buber points to reciprocity when he says that "men need, and it is granted to them, *to confirm one another* in their individual being by means of genuine meetings."[5] However, Benjamin's psychoanalytic description provides a more thorough explanation of an economy of reciprocity. Central to Benjamin's project is showing, in psychological detail, the logic of reciprocity. Or, to use Buber's terminology, Benjamin details the specific psychological reasons that "men need, and it is granted to them, to confirm one another." Benjamin's discursive community of psychoanalysis provides a detailed description of the psychological workings of reciprocity that departs from Buber's description.[6] So while reciprocity is insisted on in Buber's project, Benjamin's work offers a more robust analysis of exactly how the encounter might involve both give and take from each party.

A discursive conception of the encounter, such as the one with Kate Evans that was examined in the previous chapter is, in some ways, concerned with reciprocity. A discursive account tends to the give-and-take within the encounter, but it does so only on a discursive plane. A discursive account ultimately does not speak to how people need to act toward one another, nor does it speak to the practices of people who are involved in reciprocity; it speaks instead to the larger discursive situation of reciprocity. I include here a brief account of discursive reciprocity, although the bulk of this chapter will be concerned with how people might practice reciprocity with one another.

As an example of discursive reciprocity, I look to the work of Louis Althusser upon which Judith Butler draws. An Althusserian encounter in the classroom goes like this:[7]

A teacher is calling roll for the first time.

Teacher: Johny Abrahams?

Student: Here.

In this, the school year's first encounter between the teacher and Johny, it seems that the teacher is trying to recognize her student, Johny Abrahams. The teacher wants to know who Johny Abrahams is, so she calls his name. One way of interpreting this encounter is that Johny is gaining recognition in this public space of the classroom. Being named in the classroom, Johny can now begin to forge a public identity therein. He now has a public facet of self that has been recognized. Following this interpretation, it would seem that this recognition of Johny by his teacher is pretty much a one-way street.

However, as Althusser illustrates, being hailed is a more complicated phenomenon than this one-way interpretation indicates. Especially in the school, which is, in Althusser's terms, an "ideological state apparatus," there is a reciprocal economy of recognition. Johny is not only being recognized by his teacher. He has himself raised his hand to indicate that he recognizes his place as a student in a classroom where the teacher has the power to do the naming. To use Althusser's term, Johny has already been "interpellated" into an institutional position of subordination to the authority of the teacher. Calling of the roll assigns Johny a role. Before Johny has had the opportunity to define for himself who he will be in this public space of the classroom, he has already become subordinated to a set of institutional regulations that, laterally, set the parameters for who he can be in the classroom. As he is recognized in the roll, he recognizes his role. Recognition is practiced *by* at the same time that it is practiced *on*.

The psychoanalytic work of Jessica Benjamin and the poetry of Langston Hughes together offer a powerful description of the practice of reciprocity. The rest of this chapter will deal with the work of these two theorists. I will use Benjamin's and Hughes's works to think through the economy of reciprocity. I begin by detailing the theoretical underpinnings of Benjamin's reciprocity. Benjamin's reciprocity is a useful tool for thinking about educational scenarios such as the one in Hughes's poem, but this tool of reciprocity is more richly useful when we take the time to detail its complex psychoanalytic underpinnings. Once these complex underpinnings have been explicated, I will draw a few simple conclusions from Benjamin's project. From there, I will visit Hughes's poem in order to show the specific ways that Hughes's poetic theorizing investigates reciprocity in a school scenario.[8] Thinking with both Benjamin and Hughes, our discussion will finally turn to some general educational implications of the reciprocal encounter.

The Intrapsychic and the Intersubjective

As outlined earlier, Jessica Benjamin takes up the Hegelian problematic of reciprocity at the level of the psyche. She explains that "what Hegel formulated at the level of philosophical abstraction can also be discussed in terms of what we now know about the psychological development of the infant [and of adults]."[9]

While I have already sketched out the motivation behind Benjamin's psychoanalytic thinking on reciprocity, I want to get clearer about her fault-line account of reciprocity by limning her unique understanding of the double life of self. Since there is *intrapsychic* space and *intersubjective* space, a person can establish bonds with an other either inwardly or outwardly. Inwardly, there are images, representations, mental figures, and unconscious imaginings that I may have of another person. These inward holdings exist in intrapsychic space. As Benjamin describes intrapsychic space, it is

> the inner world of fantasy, wish, anxiety, and defense; of bodily symbols and images whose connection defy the ordinary rules of logic and language. In the inner world, the subject incorporates and expels, identifies with and repudiates the other, not as a real being, but as a mental object.[10]

The bonds formed in intrapsychic space are based on my ego's needs and drives, or based on my own way of understanding the world.

In contrast to the bonds formed in intrapsychic space are the bonds formed in intersubjective space. These bonds are exterior to the self. These bonds are experienced during fleshly encounters with the other. As Benjamin explains, intersubjectivity "refers to that zone of experience in which the other is not merely the object of the ego's need/drive or cognition/perception but has a separate and equivalent center of self."[11] An intersubjective bond is established when I interact with an other who is *not* under my control, who is radically separate from me. Whereas the intrapsychic bond involves internal, psychic manipulation of the other, the intersubjective bond involves recognition of the other as a subject with agency. Between the intrapsychic and the intersubjective, between inner and outer, lies a fault line that separates what is under my control from what is not.

Recognition, argues Benjamin, is a movement on the fault line between the inner and the outer. For a humanly fruitful event of recognition to occur, the one-recognized must himself let the other exist as truly other. If I am to be acknowledged in a way that will count, I must "destroy" my own psychic manipulation of the other and allow the other to exist on her own.[12] The other who recognizes me must be to some extent out of my intrapsychic control if she is to confirm upon me recognition that counts. As Benjamin puts it, "The being whose recognition of me is going to count for me must be one that I recognize as human."[13] The other-who-recognizes must exist in the outer space that is not under the self's control. There must be a movement on the fault line, a movement that distinguishes the other as being part of an intersubjective bond instead of an intrapsychic one, if recognition is to count. "This distinction between inner and outer reality," writes Benjamin, "is crucial to perceiving the other as a separate person."[14] Only a separate person can recognize me.

Reciprocity occurs because there must be a movement of recognizing the one-recognizing as a separate and equal center of self. If the other is to be a real other who can recognize me fruitfully, then I must, in turn, recognize her existence as separate from my own. As Hans-Georg Gadamer has put it, recognition "is only possible as double."[15] Recognition must be practiced by both sides of the self–other pair. Each side of the self–other pair must recognize in her counterpart an other who is to some extent out of the intrapsychic control of self. Self and other must be mutually recognized in intersubjective space as selves who are "separate and equivalent." There is thus an economy of recognition: If recognition is to be successful, even the one-recognized must be a one-recognizing.

Thus, according to Benjamin, the double constitution of self, with its inner and outer lives, does not just facilitate reciprocity, it also sets up the need for reciprocity. Because the psychic side of the self can take over at the expense of the intersubjective side, our own imaginings are in danger of monopolizing the event of recognition. If, for instance, I am recognized by an other without recognizing the other in return, then the one-recognizing remains largely under my own inner control. It is not healthy for me to keep the one-recognizing under my ego-driven, psychic control. If there comes a day when I must in fact engage with that other in the flesh as other, then I will not be able to reconcile my rigid intrapsychic image of her with the reality that she is indeed autonomous and not under my control. Retroactively, the recognition that I have been granted will seem insignificant, because it will be revealed as recognition that has come mostly from my own imaginings.

If I am to be recognized in a way that will be conducive to my own self-flourishing, I must acknowledge the separate existence of the one-recognizing. That requires that I let the other exist outside of my intrapsychic control. Recognition needs to be reciprocally negotiated, along the fault line of inner and outer selves, in order for recognition to be meaningful.

Benjamin's reciprocal description of the encounter, influenced as it is by the inner and outer facets of self, also points to the centrality of recognition for living a balanced life vis-à-vis the other. As Benjamin argues, the ongoing tension between inner and outer, which is tied to the reciprocal encounter between self and other, is necessary in order to avoid domination and submission. For example, domination is the most likely result of an intrapsychic life that has not acknowledged the reality of the other. If I cannot reconcile my own rigid images of an other with his actual "equivalent center of self," then I am likely to impose my own rigid images on that person. I will attempt to dominate that person in order to remain self-secure.

Conversely, if I am constantly subject to the vicissitudes of otherness, then I will come to feel as if my relationship with that person will never be under my control. Submission results as the self creates a vacuum where psychic autonomy had been. Following Benjamin, the only way to avoid domination and submission is to practice life in a way that balances intrapsychic and intersubjective experiences. In order for the psyche to find stability, it needs to practice vulnerability. Psychic stability comes from robust intrapsychic life, but it must be accompanied by a vulnerability that comes through renewed interaction with the other. Stability must be cultivated, and vulnerability risked, if domination and submission are to be avoided.

Benjamin's description of reciprocal recognition and her description of the human project of avoiding domination/submission are based on her account of psychological development. She looks to the earliest of childhood bonds to observe the stirrings of reciprocity. Very early in life, argues Benjamin, children learn to cultivate stability while risking vulnerability. When the young child looks for assurance and acknowledgment from her caretaker, she begins to learn that there is an inside and an outside to the self. Looking to a parent, the child recognizes the caretaker as partly within and partly outside her control. Benjamin explains that "the mother cannot (and should not) be a mirror; she must not merely reflect back what the child asserts; she must embody something of the not-me; she must be an independent other who responds in her different way."[16] When a child looks to a caretaker for recognition, he or she must see that the caretaker is not merely a giver of care, but is also a person with an independent life that is, to some extent, beyond the child's control. Only as independent other does the caretaker qualify as part of an outer life that is independent of the child's inner manipulations. Only as independent other can the caretaker grant recognition to the child that will help her negotiate the problematic poles of dominance and submission.

According to Benjamin, the human project of reciprocity and the avoidance of dominance/submission should be actively pursued from infancy throughout adulthood. The project of reciprocity does not end. This ongoing quality of reciprocal recognition is in stark contrast to the teleological view of recognition that is described by Freud's intrapsychic view of psychoanalysis. Freud's view of recognition is teleological insofar as it builds toward a certain end. For Freud, struggles for recognition pretty much rigidify around a constellation of events such as the oedipal struggle, gender differentiation, and a forced transition into heterosexuality. Benjamin, on the other hand, describes recognition as an ongoing project that has no specific goal or end point. As long as one continues to encounter otherness, there will be opportunities for reciprocity, for struggle, and for trade-offs between stability and vulnerability.

In fact, Benjamin's fault-line description of reciprocity suggests that recognition cannot be practiced in a fruitful way unless it continues over time. If, for example, I am a student in school who desires recognition from a teacher, one instance of recognition will not suffice over a long span of time. An initial instance of recognition, even if reciprocal and thus fruitful, can after a period of time become rigidified as a memory of how I was recognized at that time and on that particular day. As time passes, as I change, as circumstances change, I may come to doubt the value of a recognitive encounter that is not renewed. Just as I may begin to doubt the feelings of a friend whom I have not heard from for quite some time—even though our last encounter was friendly—so too a recognitive hiatus may serve to undermine the initial event of reciprocity.

In sum, Benjamin's work on reciprocity and the avoidance of domination/submission can be boiled down to three themes. First of all, Benjamin's description of reciprocity encourages acknowledgment not only of the one-recognized, but also of the one-recognizing. The identity position of the one-recognizing is central in Benjamin's account. The event of recognition must reflect not only the person who seeks recognition (as was the case, for example, in Taylor's conception of mirroring), but it must also reflect the specificity of the one who grants recognition. The one-recognizing must be acknowledged by the one-recognized as an independent center of self. The one-recognizing must be recognized as an other whose "alterity" is unique.

Second, Benjamin's account renders the encounter as an active practice. Recognition is not born solely out of a passive need for dignity or acknowledgment. Nor does it take place solely in the heads of individuals. Rather, the encounter is an active practice that contributes to habits and dispositions. It entails experiencing the reality of the other in the flesh. That the encounter is actively practiced is clear even as the first bonds of love are sought by the infant. Moreover, the practice of recognition must be actively pursued if the inhumane poles of domination/submission are to be avoided. The active practice of recognition yields dispositions that contribute to a more humane society.

Third, Benjamin's emphasis on fault-line reciprocity provides a description of recognition as an ongoing project. Benjamin theorizes recognition as a give-and-take process that occurs again and again throughout the lives of individuals.[17] For Benjamin, the encounter is a repetitive project. Reciprocity is an extension of previous reciprocal encounters. Not only does the self seek reciprocal recognition from new others, but reciprocity must be renewed on an ongoing basis even with those from whom fruitful recognition has already been attained. To borrow a phrase from the social sciences, recognition needs to be longitudinal.

Langston Hughes's Educational Contribution

To unpack the educational importance of Benjamin's conception of reciprocity, I look back to Hughes's "Theme for English B." Hughes's poem serves to map reciprocal recognition onto the domain of education. The poem begins like this:

> The instructor said,
> *Go home and write*
> *a page tonight.*
> *And let that page come out of you—*
> *Then, it will be true.*
> I wonder if it's that simple?
> I am twenty-two, colored, born in Winston-Salem.
> I went to school there, then Durham, then here
> to this college on the hill above Harlem.
> I am the only colored student in my class.
> The steps from the hill lead down into Harlem,
> through a park, then I cross St. Nicholas,
> Eighth Avenue, Seventh, and I come to the Y,
> the Harlem Branch Y, where I take the elevator
> up to my room, sit down, and write this page:

From its beginning, "Theme for English B" shows that some school assignments must be construed in terms of reciprocal recognition. His poem is a detailed study of his own struggle for recognition in a college classroom where he is the only African American student. Throughout the poem, Hughes engages in the recognitive give-and-take between stability and vulnerability. It is a nuanced struggle between the world that he has inhabited and the white classroom where he has been asked to say something about himself.

I want to start by following the progression of the poem, and will end up by linking this narrative to issues of reciprocity. The poem opens with instructions about how the student is to write a "true" assignment. As the instructor says, "Let that page come out of you— / Then, it will be true." The rest of the poem is largely a comment on the naiveté of the instructor's words. The instructor naively thinks that the student can accurately reflect on his own identity without recourse to others. He thinks that the student can write something "true" about his own identity in isolation, and that such a piece of reflective writing will have to do only with the student. Hughes's poem serves to highlight the hoodwinked perspective from which such a set of instructions is launched. The instructor says these words as if the classroom is not a space of recognition.[18]

When the student asks, "I wonder if it's that simple?" the answer that is implied in the poem is a resounding "No." The instructor's words are not only simple, they are simplistic. Yet, as readers of this poem, and as educators, we must wonder how often such naive instructions are offered in the classroom. The instructor's words are stereotypical and they are familiar. While the poem may prove them to be simplistic, they are instructions of a sort that one might well hear in a composition class. The instructor's words are simple and simplistic because they do not take into account the significance of the classroom encounter. They are simple precisely because who the student is, is not defined solely within the boundaries of the "you" that the instructor evokes when he says, "Let that page come out of you."[19]

As the poem continues, Hughes points out a number of geographical and social factors that interfere with how that page might come solely out of him. Because the milieu of the classroom is white and northern, the instructor is not likely to have much access to the life of a young black student "born in Winston-Salem," who "went to school there, then Durham," who is "the only colored student" in the class. Moreover, he is not likely to know about the student's home life. He does not know about the nightly trek that leads

> down into Harlem,
> through a park, then I cross St. Nicholas,
> Eighth Avenue, Seventh, and I come to the Y,
> the Harlem Branch Y.

Quite simply (quite simplistically), the "you" evoked by the instructor must be a falsified "you" because he does not have a clue about this student who is so different from the instructor and from the other students in his class.

Hughes's poem is not only a lament about the simplicity of the instructor's words. Ignoring the individualizing instructions of the teacher, the student uses his assignment as a springboard for investigating his own identity in light of his social circumstances. The poem continues:

It's not easy to know what is true for you or me
at twenty-two, my age. But I guess I'm what
I feel and see and hear, Harlem, I hear you:
hear you, hear me—we two—you, me, talk on this page.
(I hear New York, too.) Me—who?
Well, I like to eat, sleep, drink, and be in love.
I like to work, read, learn, and understand life.
I like a pipe for a Christmas present,
or records—Bessie, bop, or Bach.
I guess being colored doesn't make me *not* like
the same things other folks like who are other races.

So will my page be colored that I write?
Being me, it will not be white.
But it will be
a part of you, instructor.
You are white—
yet a part of me, as I am a part of you.
That's American.
Sometimes perhaps you don't want to be a part of me.
Nor do I often want to be a part of you.
But we are, that's true!
As I learn from you,
I guess you learn from me—
although you're older—and white—
and somewhat more free.

This is my page for English B.[20]

Hughes makes the assignment into an event of recognition even though the instructor's words ignore the recognitive dimension of this assignment. He disregards the emptiness of the instructor's words and creates a conversation between himself and his surroundings.

Harlem, I hear you:
hear you, hear me—we two—you, me, talk on this page.
(I hear New York, too.) Me—who?

This conversation between the student and his surroundings is no longer the monologic page that the instructor asked for. Rather, it is a give-and-take between himself and his surroundings that allows him to be both "I" and "me," both subject and object. It allows him to ask the quintessentially recognitive question: "Me—who?"

And more important for the purposes of this study of reciprocity, the poem's alternation between the "me" and the "I" highlights the back-and-forth movement of classroom recognition. Hughes's student insists on being not only the object of recognition but the subject of recognition as well—not only the "me" but also the "I." Hughes points out the activity required, on the part of the one-recognized, if the event of recognition is to be one that counts.

Hughes highlights reciprocity again as he directs his verse toward the instructor himself. The poem circles back to the instructor and refuses to let him off the hook so easily. Having just considered his own geographical and social circumstances, the student calls the instructor back. "You are white—/yet a part of me, as I am a part of you." The student calls him back in spite of the instructor's simplistic otherness. Hughes's insightful reinvocation of the instructor is another educational reminder that recognition is necessarily reciprocal if it is to be fruitful. The struggle of recognition that Hughes writes of in this poem was set in motion by the lopsided instructions of the instructor—"Let that page come out of you." However, that same struggle must call the one-recognizing back if the event is to continue. The one-recognizing must also be recognized, even if such reciprocity requires vulnerability or hard feelings. Or, as Hughes puts it,

> Sometimes perhaps you don't want to be a part of me.
> Nor do I often want to be a part of you.
> But we are, that's true.

The instructor is necessarily implicated during the event of student recognition.

Moreover, the student's activity, his agentive role in the reciprocal encounter, is further emphasized as the student notes the centrality of his own bodily circumstances. The student in Hughes's poem knows that recognition has everything to do with where he, concretely, walks ("The steps from the hill lead down into Harlem"), whose company he keeps ("I am the only colored student in my class"), what his senses take in ("I guess I'm what I feel and see and hear"), what spaces he has occupied in the past ("born in Winston-Salem./I went to school there, then Durham"). These circumstances all go into the mix when it comes to what sort of recognition can be practiced through the writing of a page for, and of, the instructor. Where the student goes in the flesh, and whom he bumps up against, are central to his recognitive experience and central to how it can be articulated in the classroom. The student is not a passive receptacle but an embodied agent whose position counts during this encounter.

Hughes's most poignant, and most painful, insight into reciprocity is found in the poem's penultimate lines. Having turned his gaze back onto the instructor, the student notes that:

> As I learn from you,
> I guess you learn from me—
> although you're older—and white—
> and somewhat more free.

Age, race, and social opportunity are three factors, among others, that underwrite recognitive reciprocity. They also underwrite who learns and who doesn't.[21] Prejudice and social constraint may go unspoken when recognition is couched in monologic terms, when the one-recognizing remains unavailable for comment or gives simplistic instructions. However, when reciprocity is demanded and the one-recognizing is himself recognized, then the discursive and material constraints that produce racism can become apparent. They can be brought into the light of day and identified as problems that require social change.

RECIPROCITY IN THE CLASSROOM

Guided by this recognitive vision of Hughes's text, I want to make some broad claims about an educational project of reciprocal recognition that dovetails with Benjamin's psychoanalytic insights. First of all, Hughes points out the significance of position for educators who are the ones-recognizing. There is an educational sleight-of-hand going on in "Theme for English B" that happens all too often. The sleight-of-hand is that the instructor acts as if student recognition does not have to do with himself as the one-recognizing, or with the educational circumstances that are a part of the encounter. In fact, for recognition in the classroom to count, the one-recognizing must also be recognized. As Hughes points out when he wonders "if it is that simple," educators are implicated in circuits of recognition. The educator's position must not be ignored.

Second, Hughes describes school as a place where recognition can be actively practiced by students. In stark contrast, for example, to Taylor's description of multicultural mirroring wherein students find their reflections in texts, Hughes's "Theme for English B" depicts a student who actively creates his own recognitive scenario. In Hughes's description of the school, recognition is not conferred upon the student as much as the student looks to his own surroundings and calls out to those whom he would like to join in the reciprocal event of recognition. The student uses his assignment to engage in a struggle of recognition. The event is not prearranged by insertion of a representational curriculum, nor is the event predicated upon the teacher's positive acknowledgment. The student takes an active role by turning his assignment into an instance of reciprocity. An educational project of recognition calls for activity—and not just passivity—on the part of students.

Third, Hughes's "Theme for English B" maps the longitudinal project of reciprocity onto the educational domain. Significantly, the student's "page" is part of an educational economy that, while it has its points of respite, is bound to continue circulation as the school year continues. What I mean is that the page itself, while it is being typed up in Harlem Branch Y, is temporarily fixed. The student has made his statement: "This is my page for English B." He is sitting in his room, some distance from school. However, he will no doubt return to school the following day. The page is, after all, not only for himself but it is also for the instructor. It will be given to the instructor, who will read it and will most probably be himself provoked when he reads lines such as "Nor do I often want to be a part of you." The fixedness of the student's page will not remain fixed for long, as the instructor will certainly react in some way or another, whether it be by some kind or not so kind words, or by the grade that he gives the student. Certainly, the instructor will assert an unexpected otherness of some sort that will serve to keep the economy of recognition moving.

Benjamin's description of reciprocal recognition, together with Hughes's mapping of that description onto the educational domain, offers a picture of the classroom as a space of lived experience. In this space, the student is not given only ameliorative images of who she is, nor is the student given only positive acknowledgment by a teacher who can accept her regardless of her identity position, nor is self-recognition only a place marker for a larger cultural conversation. In this space, the three attri-butes of reciprocity that we have looked at—recognizing the one-recog-nizing, practicing recognition actively, and recognizing over time—contribute to a sense of dignity in the public space of the classroom. They contribute also to the ability to live one's life without domination of, or submission to, others.

Practicing Reciprocity in Schools

Keeping in mind the description of the reciprocal encounter that Benja-min and Hughes outline, I would say that school is an ideal milieu for practicing such recognition. At school, students and teachers are bound to encounter others who are not like themselves. Such encounters are the stuff of reciprocity; they provide the opportunity to practice treading the fault line between intrapsychic and intersubjective experience. The school is a place where students and teachers can practice vulnerability in an environment that is relatively secure. While there is great human differ-ence within schools, schools are places where students and teachers can be protected from the extreme results of encounters that lead to physical or psychological violence. Although there are many public places, the school is a special place where one can practice the encounter under cir-cumstances that are different from the encounters one might have, say, on the street. In schools, there are figures of authority who can afford protec-tion while stability is being risked.

What's more, most schools have a rhythm whereby students go home and then return to school the next day. Such a rhythm is conducive to the give-and-take between stability and vulnerability that is necessary for cultivating fruitful recognition. At home, students and teachers experi-ence less tension as significant others are easier to anticipate, less "other." Home circumstances are often more comfortable and secure. The home provides a certain amount of stability and shelter from threatening oth-ers.[22] When students and teachers go to school, though, circumstances are less homogenous. Others will be encountered who are drastically differ-ent yet demand recognition anyway. The school is a place where one can practice recognition of others who have, in Benjamin's terms, "a separate and equivalent center of self."[23] Practicing such recognition can be threat-ening, but because the school day ends, and because students and teach-ers can go back to the private arena periodically, there will be time to be less threatened as well. Given the rhythm of schooling, students and teachers can practice both stability and vulnerability.

Tired Critiques of Psychoanalysis

Should the perspective of Benjamin be included in a work such as this that purports to link individual struggles for dignity with larger struggles for social justice? This long-standing critique of psychoanalysis—that it fails to account for structural oppression—is too worn-out for the purposes of this work for a couple of reasons. First, it is time that people get over the fear of what is inside the head. The most common refrain of the tired critique is that psychoanalysis is solely "within the heads of individuals," while ideological or class-based critiques are wider in scope, less solipsistic. Such an either–or understanding of theory—that it either looks into the heads of individuals to the exclusion of social structure or it looks at class-based struggle to the exclusion of the individual psyche—does not take into account the ways that various theoretical viewpoints can be taken up shiftingly in digital as opposed to analog fashion. As I have argued earlier, a perspectival understanding of theory, such as the one I am undertaking, highlights multiple perspectives in order become more facile at switching back and forth between them. The usefulness of psychoanalytic theory thus lies partly in its insight into the head, and partly in one's ability to code-switch to other, more class-based understandings when appropriate. The tired critique assumes that one takes psychoanalysis as a grand narrative to the exclusion of other theories. That critique is afraid of what is in the head because it assumes that it's all-in-the-head or nothing.

What's more, the process of using one's head to recognize another is ultimately a practice, and to the extent that it is a practice it provides specific opportunities to think about how societal and institutional structures interfere with or support such a practice. As Benjamin contests with her bipolar understanding of the intrapsychic and the intersubjective, psychoanalytic thinking is just as much about events of meeting as it is about what's inside the head. What happens inside the head must be installed during the practice of the encounter. The encounter, in turn, depends upon societal and institutional circumstances by which it is allowed or disallowed. By thinking clearly about the practice of intersubjective recognition, one can speak more clearly to the kinds of structures that are necessary to support such affirmation. The practice of recognition requires structural empowerments in the same way that economic distribution does. Recognitive psychoanalysis ultimately asks for nonhead results.

Schools Are Not Yet a Place of Reciprocity

Unfortunately, while schools are an ideal venue for practicing recognitive reciprocity, many schools are not in a position to encourage such a practice at present. I see two main factors deterring educators from encouraging recognitive reciprocity. One has to do with the discourses that are already in play when the school is considered a place where social and cultural differences are seriously considered. The other has to do with what Michel Foucault has called the "disciplinary apparatus" of school.[24]

Reciprocal Recognition

I have already discussed the way that educational discourses surrounding the school as a public space do not address the recognitive needs of students, nor do they address the need for individuals to practice recognition. The public space of school is often construed in terms of students who need to overcome differences, not recognize them. In the words of Nancy Fraser, who does not think that difference should be ignored, the school is often considered "a space where extant status distinctions are bracketed and neutralized."[25] Alternatively, Benjamin Barber notes that school is "our sole *public* resource: the only place where, as a collective, self-conscious public pursuing common goods, we try to shape our children to live in a democratic world."[26] Barber encourages children to pursue commonality instead of encouraging them to risk vulnerability in the pursuit of recognition of difference. When students encounter one another in schools, it is often recommended that they ignore, as opposed to recognizing and acknowledging, their human differences. Such recommendations miss Benjamin's insight that the practice of reciprocal recognition can help to cultivate the ability to maintain balanced relationships. To ignore the cultivation of this ability is to neglect to educate.

Ironically, much discussion of multicultural education pays little attention to how actual bodies need to practice reciprocal recognition. This is ironic because multicultural education is, in the end, all about how people of diverse cultures need to interact with one another. When discussion of multicultural education stays at the textual level of transforming curriculum and diversifying content, then the crucial matter of how recognition gets practiced in the flesh is overlooked. While a transformational curriculum may empower students because it reflects well on a student's particular culture, and because it gives voice to the heretofore unvoiced, such curricular change does not speak to the psychological habits that need to be cultivated if students and teachers are to actually learn to recognize one another. I find this lack of thinking about the "practicing self" disturbing. The public space of schools is a concrete place; students and teachers go there in the flesh. They learn to act in certain ways with others. They learn to associate with certain people, and sometimes not with others. They form habits. As long as educational discourses ignore the practice of recognition, there will be little chance for educators to think about, let alone encourage and facilitate, students and teachers acquiring habits of reciprocity.

Moreover, as Donna Kerr has argued, much current rhetoric about "democratic education" does not speak to the practice of interaction between self and other. Such rhetoric seems to ignore the fact that civil society must flourish among real people who have real differences. As Kerr explains,

> Rhetoric that considers schooling instrumental to civil society—which, in turn, is instrumental to democracy—misses a fundamental moral point. If persons live in relationships of domination and subservience, no rhetoric of democracy can render their relations democratic.[27]

I take this to mean that it is a mistake to hollow out the important signifier "democracy" to such an extent that it no longer speaks to how individuals actually are with each other. If the impassioned rhetoric of "democratic education" cannot speak to the habits between self and other, then what rhetoric will? It is similarly the case with public rhetoric and with multicultural rhetoric. All of these discourses address the crucial matter of difference, but they do not always address the matter of how diverse people need to be with one another.

"Disciplinary" Discouragement of Reciprocity

In addition to educational discourses that do not address the practice of recognitive reciprocity, Michel Foucault's work on the disciplinary tendencies of schools shows how the day-to-day workings of schools actually discourage self–other recognition at present. Within the disciplinary regime of schools, the practice of recognition is discouraged in at least four ways: through grouping, through ranking, through individuation, and through self-monitoring. Also, Foucault's work on the disciplinary constitution of self shows that such discouragement extends beyond the immediate purview of the school and into society at large.

Many educational practices discourage students from encountering otherness. One such practice is the grouping of students. Ability grouping, age differentiation, tracking of athletes, tracking of honors students, tracking of students with "discipline problems"—all of these limit the extent to which students can interact. Ironically, grouping will sometimes foil the practice of intersubjective recognition even when the official curriculum of a school seems intended to bolster recognition. For instance, it is still the case in many magnet schools that students will be bused into a school, ostensibly to encourage cross-cultural interaction, only to be grouped into courses whose student makeup is just as homogeneous as the neighborhoods from which those students are bused.

The ranking of students similarly detracts from a project of intersubjective recognition. By ranking, I mean the way that students are situated in hierarchies that differentiate each student from every other student. While ranking does create a situation where individuals are situated in a relation of difference to each other, such difference is hierarchical and objectified—it is not the stuff of recognition. Ranking hearkens back to the kind of difference that Charles Taylor describes as "honor"—a ranking that is not conducive to recognizing an other because one person's honor comes at the expense of another person's.

Individuation is another educational device that keeps people from practicing intersubjective recognition. As Foucault points out, one of the great innovations of disciplinary power is the creation of "cells."[28] Cells are those interchangeable units like desks, cubicles, listening stations, exercise stations, and computer terminals. In cells, students are kept busy and by themselves, occupied and individuated. In cells, there is little chance to encounter the other.

Self-monitoring, or "panopticism," is another institutional practice that keeps individuals from practicing intersubjective recognition.[29] Using the metaphor of Jeremy Bentham's panopticon, Foucault describes the way that modern institutions encourage individuals to patrol themselves. Modern power, says Foucault, encourages the individual to patrol herself much like the prison inmate who acts well because she is not sure who is watching her. Thus, students and teachers keep themselves in line. They spend much time making sure that the self stays within limits of institutional acceptability. When one is focused on self-conduct, there will be little attention paid to the self–other relation that is central to recognition.

It is hard to disagree with Foucault about the degree to which grouping, ranking, individuation, and self-monitoring pervade educational institutions. His description must ring true to just about anyone who has spent time in large classrooms. From the point of view of this study, these practices of the self deter students and teachers from practicing intersubjective recognition. The above disciplinary measures create a performative contradiction when it comes to the public space of school. On the one hand, diverse students are brought together to interact in the public space of school. On the other, the very disciplinary measures that keep the school running smoothly ensure that students will not interact with otherness. In schools, homogeneity is the rule. Reciprocal recognition cannot be practiced when institutional practices encourage encounters with sameness and not difference.

Even more serious, though, is Foucault's assertion that disciplinary power produces individuals. That is to say, Foucault argues that the school is not only a temporary apparatus that constrains individuals for a bit, only to let them interact normally thereafter. Rather, schools act to produce individuals who in turn conduct their own lives by means of such disciplinary norms. The school produces the expectations of what interaction "normally" means.

As Foucault says,

> it's my hypothesis that the individual is not a pre-given entity which is seized on by the exercise of power. The individual, with his identity and characteristics, is the product of a relation of power exercised over bodies, multiplicities, movements, desires, forces.[30]

More serious than the disciplinary practices of schools are the modes of self-conduct that are produced by those disciplinary practices. Foucault tells us that institutions such as schools establish ways of self-conduct and interaction that become the norm in the larger society. Such a production of self-conduct is a very serious matter if selves are being disciplined away from practicing reciprocal recognition. It is serious because not practicing recognition leads to an inability to deal with that which is other. Not practicing reciprocal recognition can lead the self into circuits of domination and submission with otherness. If Foucault is even close to being correct in his assessment of the institutional production of the individual, then the way students learn to conduct themselves vis-à-vis otherness, the way they learn to act or not interact, sets the stage for how humans will conduct themselves in all spheres of life.

Overcoming Drawbacks to Reciprocity

In short, the deterrents to the educational practice of recognitive reciprocity are both rhetorical and institutional. With regard to the former, my aim here is to add to the rhetoric of education in such a way that the practice of recognition will be brought to the attention of educators. I want to show that recognition and, in particular, the reciprocal practice of recognition, are concepts "upon which we can ride." I am trying to show that an educational rhetoric that includes reciprocity is substantive enough to deserve consideration.

With regard to the institutional deterrents to reciprocity, I would say that Foucault's insights are both discouraging and encouraging. They are discouraging insofar as he is able to point out so vividly how schools produce individuals who are concerned more with atomistic habits of self that are not reciprocal than with the practice of intersubjective recognition. But Foucault's observations are encouraging insofar as they point to the sorts of classroom configurations and educational practices that need to be revamped if reciprocal recognition is to be practiced. They are also encouraging because they offer the hope that schools can partake in the production of selves who practice reciprocity as a way of life. One of Foucault's most encouraging, and sobering, observations is that the individual is produced by disciplinary power. Schools shape selves; schools can shape the way humans interact.

By pointing to specific school practices such as grouping, ranking, individuation, and self-monitoring, Foucault identifies the educational arrangements that need to be reconfigured if educators are going to encourage intersubjective habits of self-conduct, as opposed to individualistic ones. From a recognitive point of view, it is imperative to think not how students can most efficiently be arranged and ordered, but how students can most effectively be encouraged to practice reciprocal recognition. At specific times during the school day, arrangement and ordering should be subordinated to creating space for reciprocal recognition between students. In short, schools can, and should, create spaces that encourage interaction between self and other. In such places, habits of recognition, instead of habits of individuation, could be learned.

Some people might say there is already time allotted during the school day for reciprocal recognition. For example, students and teachers can interact with whomever they choose during lunch periods, during breaks, and after school. But this sort of interaction is more likely to reproduce whatever habits of self-conduct are already at work. It is not likely that people will risk vulnerability during such times, nor that they will be willing to encounter the other as "an equivalent and equal center of self." Recognition does not come that easily.

On the contrary, recognition is too difficult and complex a practice to happen automatically, whenever self and other meet. The practice of recognition is important enough, difficult enough, and complex enough to require educational intervention. The school needs to be a place where students and teachers can practice confronting others who are, perhaps, threatening. There need to be orchestrated opportunities for reciprocal encounters, for vulnerability and risk-taking. Teachers and administrators should provide safe spaces for such encounters. To provide such spaces, educators should de-emphasize grouping, ranking, individuation, and self-monitoring during certain parts of the school day in order to shift student attention toward the encounter. In Hughes's words, there need to be times when one person can say to another, "perhaps you don't want to be a part of me./Nor do I often want to be a part of you./But we are, that's true." Such times can help students to negotiate psychic and experiential poles of stability and vulnerability.

What I have been suggesting in this chapter is that the encounter is a habit as well as an event. By that I mean that the self–other encounter is not only about how texts, acknowledgment, and interpretation affect one person, it is also about how texts, acknowledgment, and interpretation are used by two human agents who are in relation. The habit of the encounter, considered in light of Benjamin's psychoanalytic description of reciprocity, requires at least three things: that the position of the one-recognizing be acknowledged, that the one-recognized be in a position to practice recognition actively, and that recognition be practiced over and over. The rhetoric and practice of schools need to change for these things to happen. In the next chapter, I look at one example of how educators might begin to change both rhetoric and practice to address recognition in the classroom.

NOTES

1. Franz Fanon, *Black Skins/White Masks*, translated by Charles Lam Markmann (New York: Grove Press, 1967), 217.

2. G. W. F. Hegel, *Phenomenology of Spirit*, translated by A. V. Miller (New York: Oxford University Press, 1977), 113

3. Hegel, *Phenomenology*, 111.

4. Neetha Ravjee addresses Taylor's lack of attention to the one-recognizing in her "Critical Recognition, a Framework for Access: The Case of Engineering Education," (Ph.D. diss., University of Washington, 1998), abstract in *Dissertation Abstracts International* 59 (1998): 1943A.

5. Martin Buber, *Knowledge of Man* (London: George Allen & Unwin, 1965), 69.

6. That is not to say that such workings cannot be construed from Buber's insistence on reciprocity; it is only to say that I find Benjamin's description more compelling, more of a description "upon which we can ride," to go back to William James's phrase.

7. This is a variation of Althusser's account of a policeman who "hails" a person walking along the street. Louis Althusser, "Ideology and Ideological State Apparatuses (Notes toward an Investigation)," in *Mapping Ideology*, edited by Slavoj Zizek (New York: Verso, 1994).

8. For an analysis of the hermeneutic reciprocity involved in this poem, see Charles Bingham, "The Poetic Theorizing of Langston Hughes: Curriculum and Education of Identity," *Journal of Thought* 33 (1998): 15–26.

9. Jessica Benjamin, *The Bonds of Love: Psychoanalysis, Feminism and the Problem of Domination* (New York: Pantheon, 1988), 12.

10. Benjamin, *The Bonds of Love*, 20–21.

11. Jessica Benjamin, *Like Subjects, Love Objects: Essays on Recognition and Sexual Difference* (New Haven, Conn.: Yale University Press, 1998), 30.

12. For a psychoanalytic analysis of "destruction," see D. W. Winnicott, *Playing and Reality* (New York: Routledge, 1971).

13. Charles Taylor, *Hegel* (Cambridge: Cambridge University Press, 1975), 153.

14. Benjamin, *Bonds of Love*, 213.

15. Hans-Georg Gadamer, *Hegel's Dialectic: Five Hermeneutical Studies*, translated by P. Christopher Smith (New Haven, Conn.: Yale University Press, 1976), 62.

16. Benjamin, *Bonds of Love*, 24.

17. Let me make a distinction here with regard to the repeating of the encounter. Butler focuses quite specifically on the extent to which identity is kept in play by means of its repeatability, by its "citationality." According to Butler, repeating the discursive cues of the encounter is central. However, the repeating that we will be addressing here assumes that there is also a psychological self that can be cultivated through a subjective act of repetition. So while Butler speaks of discur-

sive repetition, it is not same sort of active repetition of the intrasubjective/inter-subjective self that one finds in Benjamin.

18. Of course, strictly speaking, we do not know exactly what the instructor meant by his instructions, only how Hughes takes the assignment up.

19. I use "he" here, although we do not actually know the gender of the instructor.

20. Langston Hughes, *Selected Poems* (New York: Vintage, 1959), 247.

21. Or, to historicize this poem and thus show the "concrete" effects of the one-recognizing's power over the one-recognized, Langston Hughes indeed attended a college—Columbia—much like the one he describes in the poem, and went through struggles for recognition that are similar to those in the poem. For reasons that may be precisely those racist conditions described by the student in "English B," Hughes dropped out of Columbia after his first year. See James S. Haskins, *Always Movin' On: The Life of Langston Hughes* (Newark, N.J.: African World Press, 1993), 25.

22. It might be argued here against the scenario that I have offered that many homes lack the necessary stability to serve as a respite from encounters of otherness. See, for example, Sharon Quint, *Schooling Homeless Children: A Working Model for America's Public Schools* (New York: Teachers College Press, 1994). In response I would say that if recognition is not to be practiced in the schools, then that means giving up on the idea that schools can do anything to cultivate the positive self-image of students. Such a situation is clearly even more detrimental for students whose homes are not at all stable.

23. Benjamin, *Bonds of Love*, 30.

24. Michel Foucault, *Discipline and Punish* (New York: Vintage, 1979).

25. Nancy Fraser, *Justice Interruptus: Critical Reflections on the "Postsocialist" Condition* (New York: Routledge, 1997), 74.

26. Benjamin Barber, *An Aristocracy of Everyone* (New York: Oxford University Press, 1992), 14–15.

27. Donna Kerr, "Toward a Democratic Rhetoric of Schooling," in *The Public Purpose of Education and Schooling,* edited by John I. Goodlad and Timothy J. McMannon (San Francisco: Jossey-Bass, 1997), 78.

28. Foucault, *Discipline and Punish*, 135–169.

29. Foucault, *Discipline and Punish*, 195–228.

30. Michel Foucault, *Power/Knowledge: Selected Interviews and Other Writings 1972–1977*, edited by Colin Gordon (New York: Pantheon, 1980), 74.

6

Thinking through the Encounter: Minding Our Educational Discourses of Recognition

We have seen that several discourses of recognition provide useful ways to open up issues central to human dignity in the classroom and beyond. The encounter with the other is crucial to education because recognition can promote the flourishing of students and teachers. It is also important because it can be a heuristic device for social activism in schools. Or, tragically, misrecognition can be personally and socially oppressive and devastating for students, for teachers, and, as I show in this chapter, for parents too. I have examined various perspectives on classroom encounters, keeping in mind that encounters must be redescribed in rich and perhaps conflictual ways if educators are to approach the recognitive event in a manner nuanced enough to grapple with the complexities of human flourishing.

My analysis has kept the four discourses of recognition separate in order to emphasize the distinctly different ways that recognitive descriptions can help educators to think about classroom identities. Ultimately, though, I think that the different discourses of recognition that I have looked into form a constellation of ways to think about education and self-flourishing, and this constellation hangs together under the general rubric of a recognitive perspective. If these discourses are sometimes conflictual, so be it. Human life is conflictual. There is no reason to think that specific aspects of human life, such as the encounter, will be any less conflictual. The fact that different descriptions of the encounter are conflictual, yet useful just the same, points to the rich complexity of the encounter rather than to the failure of these descriptions. A failure of these

141

discourses might arise not because they are conflictual per se, but if such conflict got in the way of their usefulness. At this book's end, there will remain the ethical challenge for you and me to take these discourses up in ways that maximize their work in the name of dignity and social change in schools.

Together, these four recognitive descriptions contribute to an educational discourse of recognition that is particularly applicable to encounters in the public space of school. I use our four-pronged discussion of recognition to think through a classroom encounter that has recently gained widespread media attention.[1] I show how all four descriptions can be brought to bear on one classroom scenario.

THE DISCOURSES OF RECOGNITION

Here are some of the main points that can be drawn from the four discourses of recognition that I have outlined in this work, discussions that were traced back to their Hegelian roots.

Recognitive Description of the Public Sphere

Recall that such a liberal description of the encounter has the following attributes:

- The self is not atomistic, but needs special affirmation in the unfamiliar surroundings of the public arena. Specifically, students need affirmation of their cultural horizons in the public space of school. They need to be reflected well, that is to say, well recognized by others.
- Misrecognition, in the form of nonrecognition or malrecognition, is a personal affront to dignity. Such an affront should be a rallying point for social change. Such misrecognition is most appropriately articulated by the person or people whose dignity is demeaned.
- Understood recognitively, multicultural curriculum transformation is important because of its potential for "mirroring" students in uplifting ways.
- Recognition is not psychically simple. The psyche can entertain multiple identity positions at once, and such positions can be forced by racist othering.

An Existential Description of Confirmation

Buber's confirmative account underscores these issues:

- It may not be possible, or desirable, to know the other during the recognitive encounter. It is necessary to be able to confirm the other in his or her profound unknowability.
- The dialogic experience of presence before an other is central to the encounter.
- Confirmative encounters can be a means by which to surface social oppressions that need to be changed.

Recognition in Terms of Subjection

A poststructuralist account of recognition reminds us of the following:

- Recognition entails a re-cognition of cultural cues. Thus, one cannot recognize an "authentic" identity of the other. Recognition is an act of being subjected to discursive availabilities.
- The quality of recognition afforded to the one-recognized cannot be decided beforehand but must be worked out during the event. This is because the encounter itself will consist of evoking cultural conversations that go beyond the subjectivities of individuals.
- Curricular representations cannot promote recognition pure and simple. Recognition will be a matter of how curriculum is interpreted by the one-recognized.
- Strategic enactment of the encounter on the part of the one-recognized can ameliorate stereotypes and prejudiced cultural understandings.

A Redescription of the Reciprocal Encounter

This psychoanalytic perspective offers the following recognitive observations:

- The recognitive encounter will necessarily be an event where self and other risk vulnerability.
- Attention must be paid not only to the one-recognized but to the one-recognizing as well.

- The practice of reciprocal recognition helps to develop abilities of self-conduct that can help one to avoid the unfortunate poles of domination and submission.
- Practicing the encounter needs to be an ongoing project if it is going to lead to human flourishing.

These various discourses highlight, in a recognitive way, identity formation and human flourishing within the context of educational encounters. They do not form a typology, nor do they serve to cover all of the recognitive concerns that might arise in public spaces of education. Rather, these discourses shed recognitive light on various educational concerns in various ways. These discourses also do not create a scenario of recognitive relativism. Instead of offering an incoherent set of educational views onto one stable thing, recognition, these discourses highlight that *educational* recognition itself must be differently described, and differently acted upon, in different scenarios. For instance, Taylor's discourse on mirroring is particularly useful when it comes to describing, and acting upon, the public aspects of identity, identity politics, and textual representation. Buber's discourse on confirmation offers suggestions for personal contact with the other. Butler's discourse on subjection is useful for challenging the discursive debt that always accompanies the recognitive encounter. Benjamin's discourse on reciprocity reminds us to treat the encounter as an active granting of recognition. In sum, I maintain that each of these discourses lends itself most usefully to a particular understanding, and a particular educational practice, of recognition. These discrete multiple understandings add to a "perspectivist" theory, not a "relativist" one.

CLASSROOM ENCOUNTERS—*NAPPY HAIR*

Informed by the above insights into recognition, I want to examine a classroom encounter that has garnered much media attention. The recent media excitement over the classroom use of the children's book *Nappy Hair* begs for a more thorough analysis than has been rendered in the popular press.[2] I want to use a recognitive discourse to generate a more nuanced understanding of this particular encounter. Troubling the limiting descriptions that are provided by the popular press, I offer detailed attention to the *Nappy Hair* incident as an event of recognition. Such attention affords a fruitful application of this work's recognitive analysis.

This *Nappy Hair* incident and its media portrayal influenced my instruction of preservice teachers, despite the fact that I was teaching on the West Coast and the incident happened in New York. Even though my students and I were not involved directly in the *Nappy Hair* incident, its recognitive dimensions provoked us to discuss the incident at great length. The incident involving *Nappy Hair* was brought to my attention by future elementary school teachers who were concerned about what such a story meant for their own classroom practice. Specifically, they were worried that they would find themselves in a situation similar to the one they had read about in the press.

As we talked about the *Nappy Hair* event in class, I was fortunate enough to be in the midst of this project on recognition, and I found that my own research on interhuman encounters meshed with my students' concern over the incident. At the time, though, my research had not yet given me a sufficiently nuanced vocabulary for speaking to this well-publicized event. The following analysis is a by-product of my own research as well as our class discussions. Ironically, and perhaps predictably, it is only now that the course is over that I feel myself in a position to speak about this incident, now that the "teachable moment" has passed. I hope this analysis will spark thought for others who want to talk about similar themes and who are in a position to create the teachable moment that I missed.

Newsweek magazine and the *New York Times* relate the school encounter over *Nappy Hair* as it precipitously happens at PS 75 in Brooklyn, New York.[3] Ruth Sherman, a white teacher of a third-grade classroom, was a reading tutor at PS 75 during her student teaching. Because she was successful at raising the reading scores of the children with whom she worked, the school hired her on as a full-time teacher. This is her first year as a teacher, and her students are mostly African American and Hispanic.

Ms. Sherman uses all sorts of books in her classroom. One book tells the story of a Haitian child who made a doll from a broom. Another book tells of a Vietnamese girl who is teased because of her pajamalike clothes. She reads the book *Nappy Hair*, by Carolivia Herron, and the students take to the book immediately. The book tells the story of an African American girl, Brenda, who has been blessed by God with curly, "nappy," hair. As the book says, Brenda "had the kinkiest, the nappiest, the fuzziest, the most screwed-up, squeezed-up, knotted-up, tangled-up" hair. The story tells about where Brenda got this "nappy" hair and why this hair is something to be proud of. Ms. Sherman sends her students home with some photocopied pictures from the book.

Soon, there is a reaction by parents. Having seen photocopies of the book that their children have brought home, over fifty parents organize a meeting at the school to object to the book's portrayal of this African American girl. The story about nappy hair does not sit well with them. As Dennis L. Herring, school board president, put it, "When the pages were copied from the book and there was no background information explaining how it was meant, it looks like pictures to degrade African-Americans."[4] The meeting results in a confrontation between the parents and Ms. Sherman. During the meeting, some of the parents tell her, "You better watch out" and "We're going to get you."[5] They also use ethnic epithets. According to *Newsweek*, they called Ms. Sherman "cracker." Following the meeting, Ms. Sherman is escorted by security guards to her waiting husband, who has driven to the school to pick her up.

It's not just the photocopy of *Nappy Hair* that the parents find questionable. The *Nappy Hair* narrative has as its central theme the "nappy" hair of a young African American girl named Brenda. "Nappy," a term sometimes used to describe African American hair, is often used as an insult. Employing Uma Narayan's terminology, I would say it is an insider's word, a word that is best judged from the point of view of African Americans who use the term in such a way. I remember hearing the term used by my African American friends when I was an elementary school student. I remember thinking that the term was not, for me as a white person, one that I should use unless I was sure the circumstances called for its use. The parents in this incident are upset that such a term is taught in school by a white teacher.

The confrontation between Ms. Sherman and the parents leads to a change of schools for Ms. Sherman. At first, she is relocated to a desk job at the school district office, and then she decides not to go back to PS 75. She cites the parental threats as the main reason for not going back to her old classroom: "If I had not been threatened, I would have been back today."[6]

The bare bones of the *Nappy Hair* encounter were consistently rendered in the popular media, though the media also added glosses that revealed the press's sympathy for the white teacher and antipathy for the black parents. The *Newsweek* account, in particular, was laced with racist fright. Such racist fright is evident as the article recounts how the principal said that the parent group "turned into a lynch mob"—a hegemonic re-inscription of the quintessential racist moment in America. The article then notes how "Sherman was in hysterics, waiting for someone to escort her out of the neighborhood"—a description that conjures up stereotypical images of white fright upon wandering into a black neighborhood. It is there within the infantilizing suggestion that parents who have such negative reactions should "STOP! STAY CALM, LET'S WORK IT OUT," just as the poster says at the back of Ms. Sherman's third-grade classroom. The *Newsweek* article says that Ms. Sherman "was caught in the cross hairs of political correctness"—employing the conservatively charged signifier, PC, that has so often used to silence textual activism.[7]

But it is not the popular media's racism that I want to highlight. What I want to highlight are the less overtly prejudicial discourses that the media used to fill in the bare bones of this encounter. The media accounts supplied quite a few facts that were to inform readers about the book, its author, Ms. Sherman, and the parents. I include these other facts in order to show that commonsense understandings of the encounter need to be supplemented by a recognitive analysis if educators are to begin to conceptualize the public space of school in any rich way, in a way that aims to promote the dignity of students, parents, and teachers.

Here are some additional facts that were included in the media accounts. First, "the book was widely praised."[8] The *New York Times* notes that its author is a reputable scholar and that critical reception of the book has been positive. States the *Times*, "Isoke T. Nia, the director of research and development at the Teachers College Reading and Writing Project at Columbia University, who is black . . . has recommended the book to hundreds of teachers."[9] That is to say, this book was considered by many to be a good piece of multicultural literature. Moreover, the book's author, Carolivia Herron, an African American, is an assistant professor of English at California State University at Chico. She studied classical poetry (such as Homer and Ovid) as a student, and she wrote the book *Nappy Hair*, which is an extended lyric, trying to capture a certain oral style that her uncle had used during her youth. These facts work to substantiate the literary merit of the text.

Second, the book was intended to build a child's self-esteem. Ms. Herron, notes the *Times*, "has said that the teacher used the book exactly as she had intended: to celebrate racial diversity and teach children to be proud of who they are."[10] Because Ms. Sherman had intended the book as an exercise in self-esteem, she "said she was surprised by the response since it was the exact opposite of what she had hoped to achieve by distributing the book."[11] These facts work to back up the good intentions of the teacher.

Moreover, the media notes how some of the parents would not budge from their decision that *Nappy Hair* was not to their liking. Ms. Wright, one of the parents, was not satisfied that anyone had made a compelling case for the classroom use of the book. The *Times* quotes Ms. Wright as follows: "I asked [Ms. Sherman], 'Well, what was your purpose for using this book?' Ms. Wright said. 'I want to understand what you were trying to convey.' I was told, 'Well, I was trying to make her feel good about her hair.' Who said my child had problems with her hair?'"[12] This information shows how profoundly disparate Ms. Sherman's intentions were from what Ms. Wright actually wanted from her child's education.

As my preservice students and I discussed this scenario, I found that the themes touched upon by the media descriptions were echoed by my own students. My students, who were mostly white, worried about how to reconcile three important aspects of the reading material they might choose for their own classrooms: literary merit, teacher intentions, and parent reception. They were concerned about how they could choose texts that would be culturally uplifting for their students. What if they were wrong in their choices? Isn't good intention enough? Some of them were afraid that they, like Ms. Sherman, would be put in uncomfortable situations if the literature they chose turned out to be ill received by parents. It was very difficult in our classroom discussions to get out of the sort of either/or thinking that puts either the teacher or the parents on the moral high ground while blaming the other party.

Ultimately, the media representations afforded Ms. Sherman that high ground. As a compliment to my own students, I would say that they were not willing to let the matter resolve itself so simplistically. My students sensed that there were more issues involved than merit, intention, and reception. They were particularly disappointed with Ms. Sherman for leaving her teaching job, but neither my students nor I had a well-thought-out solution. At the time, I was not able to articulate my own position on the *Nappy Hair* episode as well as I would have liked. Now, having written the chapters of this work, I am better able to do so. Here I will use some of the recognitive themes outlined in this work to examine the case of *Nappy Hair*.

Mirroring and Complexity

If an analysis of recognition tells us anything about the *Nappy Hair* encounter, it tells us that public mirroring, such as that which was intended by Ms. Sherman with her classroom use of this book, is a complicated endeavor. While mirroring is a straightforward metaphor for the personal and cultural recognitions that need to take place in the public space of the school, it is also a complicated metaphor that should be employed with an eye toward its profound implications regarding the self-worth of individuals. When I look in the mirror, that image has a great impact on how I will be on that particular day and in the days to come. Mirroring is a complex phenomenon that has to do not only with superficial images but with my cultural, historical, and psychological situation. It matters not only that I have a chance to look in the mirror but also that the reflection is to my liking and to my betterment.

Likewise, it is not only that students need to find themselves represented in curricula and in school activities. Ultimately, it is also a question of how students find themselves therein. It is not just a question of whether or not there is mirroring going on in the classroom; it is also a question of whether that mirroring contributes to a sense of dignity. Mirroring can be ameliorative, or it can be, in Taylor's words, "confining or demeaning or contemptible."[13] As educators, we should remember that the phenomenon of public mirroring is bound to be more complex than a story that is narrated within the pages of a children's book.

Public Encounters and Social Change

It is also crucial to remember that the school is a public space of recognition. Whether it be students or teachers or parents who occupy that public space, it is vital that we, as educators, are prepared for recognitive encounters. As Charles Taylor points out, the recognitive dimension of the public arena is a fact of modern human existence. It should not be surprising that struggles for acknowledgment get played out in schools. The misunderstanding between the parents and Ms. Sherman was a clear case of a group of people who felt themselves misrecognized in the public space of the classroom. Because the classroom is a public space, a recognitive struggle such as this one should be expected instead of feared.

I would further say that an affront to dignity is always a valid place to begin a discussion on how to improve social conditions. It is not necessary to decide who is right or who is wrong. The very fact that there is a perceived affront to dignity must be used as a point of departure for a discussion of social improvement. The very fact that there is such a gulf between, on the one hand, a parent who is sure that her child's cultural self-concept is positive and, on the other, a teacher who assumes that her students need to have their self-esteem improved through the use of a text such as *Nappy Hair*—this very gulf should be used as a point of departure for deliberation in the public space of the school. The media representations of this incident give us a two-sided story, implying that the two sides are at odds, but a recognitive perspective would not be worried so much about the correctness of those on the two sides as about the gulf itself. In other words, I am not trying to say who is wrong or right in this scenario as much as I am trying to point out that there is a gulf that must be attended to. It is this gulf that has given rise to a struggle for recognition. If attended to, this very struggle might have started a chain of events that would lead to an improvement of social relations instead of leading to a fiasco.

Textual Interpretations

There are a few things that need to be taken into account if a scenario such as this is to have a result that is humanly helpful instead of perniciously provocative. First of all, a school curriculum must be considered not only for its *intended* value but for its *practical* value as a piece of interpreted text. Whether a particular text offers a flattering reflection cannot be decided once and for all by making the claim that it was meant by its author to be uplifting. Nor can it be determined by the reputation and qualifications of its author, nor can it be judged by the extent to which the text has garnered critical acclaim, nor can it be decided by the intention of the teacher who is using the text.

A text like *Nappy Hair* must be considered at the intersection of intention and interpretation. How one reads a text is just as important as what the author or the teacher intended to do with that text. A text cannot be separated from the way it is read. In this case, the parents who responded to *Nappy Hair* read the text in a way that needs to be respected. Their reading of the book needs to be deliberated over instead of dismissed. It needs to be a cause for discussion instead of a cause for condemnation. To ignore how a text is received is as educationally irresponsible as ignoring whether students have learned or not.

Two-Way Recognition in the Public Schools

Taking a cue from the work of Jessica Benjamin, it is also imperative to consider the position of the one-recognized. Because the encounter with the other is a matter of reciprocity, the one-recognizing cannot be left off the hook. Although it may seem that the teacher is, unilaterally, the one-recognizing in the public space of the classroom, it is essential to look into the circumstances, the identity, and the recognitive qualifications of the teacher. What makes a given teacher suited to afford recognition to students, or in this case to parents?

In the media reception of this incident, we are reminded a few times that this teacher began as a reading assistant and that she had been very successful at improving the reading scores of students at PS 75. Does the ability to improve reading scores have much to do with the ability to choose texts that will acknowledge students, or to acknowledge their parents? What does a white teacher's pedagogical adroitness have to do with her capacity to afford her African American students or their parents cultural recognition? The ability to teach cognitive skills must not be confused with the ability to affirm others in the public space of school. Recognizing the other is neither the same as, nor should it be subordinated to, knowledge transference. These two educational matters should both be the concern of educators; one should not hide in the shadow of the other.

In my own classroom of preservice teachers, this issue of the disjuncture between the twin roles of being a teacher and being the one-recognizing was raised when the students voiced their concerns with the *Nappy Hair* incident. Worried that their own efforts to infuse the curriculum with affirming images of people from cultures not their own would result in a similar confrontation, my students were worried that their teacher preparation was not training them to recognize the cultures of their own students.

I would say that their worries stemmed from the limited vocabulary of recognition that is available to educators. Matters of identity acknowledgment are too easily simplified into issues of teacher intent and curriculum choice when a discourse of recognition is not available. At present, such a discourse is not available. An incapacity to afford positive recognition must not be hidden behind the alibi of "Yes, but she is such a good teacher!" To respond to my students' concerns, I would now say that a "good" teacher has the added challenge to be a person who can encourage recognition in the public space of the classroom. Addressing that challenge means thinking about the recognitive discourses that I have addressed in this work. More specifically, it means thinking about one's own position as a teacher-who-recognizes.

Presence

Another important insight that a recognitive lens offers in the case of *Nappy Hair* is the simple lesson of being there. On a person-to-person level, one cannot confirm another if one leaves the scene. As Martin Buber puts it, the confirmative moment must include the chance for that "raising of a finger, perhaps, or a questioning glance" that is "the other half of what happens in education."[14] A teacher who wishes to engage in the public event of recognition needs to be willing to hang in there even if tempers flare and if it feels uncomfortable. In fact, the central challenge of a recognitive project is the realization that selves are malleable, needy, and susceptible in such public spaces as schools. One challenge of encountering the other is to accept that one must risk being vulnerable. While it may be easier to walk away from a tension-filled encounter, doing so means giving up recognitive aspirations.

I am reminded of Ms. Call here. While it is tempting to summarily dismiss the student who sketches a "Jew Burner 2000," and while I myself would be tempted to expel such a student from my class in order to set an example to others, a project of recognition reminds us to approach others and establish a relation just as Ms. Call did. It is within a relation of presence with the other, however uncomfortable that relation might be, that recognitive events unfold.

An Ongoing Project

Related to the matter of presence, I would point to the importance of a continual return to the recognitive scene. It is not the end of the recognitive world if a teacher chooses, initially, to leave a tension-filled situation. Not all teachers will have the personal fortitude, or the sensitivity to self–other interaction, to tolerate uncomfortableness. However, there is no excuse for giving up entirely on the educational project of recognition. The school year provides a day-to-day coming and going of students, teachers, and parents that can afford time for recognitive uncomfortableness to cool off for a bit before the encounter heats things up again. The tragedy of this episode is not so much that Ms. Sherman went home abruptly on that particular day as it is that she did not use the recognitive rhythm of the school year to engage once again with parents who sustained a personal affront to dignity. School meetings can be called again and again. Students, teachers, and parents can meet again and again. The longitudinal project of recognition requires as much.

Ironically, Ms. Sherman was accompanied away from school by a security guard. If anything, security guards are situated inside schools in order to ensure the modicum of peacefulness that was needed during this very encounter. The school should patrol its premises so that recognitive encounters do happen, not so that they do not. Schools must be safe places where the recognitive encounters are encouraged. If the well-managed space of the school cannot be a safe haven in which to negotiate the fragile poles of stability and vulnerability, then what hope is there that any public space will serve that purpose? Schools are, as Foucault points out, a place where habits of self are produced. Habits of human flourishing between self and other can be formed only if educators and students are willing to practice recognition, again and again, in public spaces like the school.

Discursive Cues

In addition to considering how important it is that teachers, students, and parents engage personally in an ongoing relation of presence, it is important to consider the larger social cues that are being enacted in this *Nappy Hair* incident. Guided by Judith Butler's lateral understanding of recognition, I have come to be suspicious of considering an incident such as this a matter that is restricted to the subjectivities of individuals. What is almost completely glossed over in the media accounts of this incident, and what was also unfortunately glossed over in the discussions that I had with my students about this classroom encounter, is any sense that a larger set of cultural cues were being enacted as the parents objected to this text.

The reaction of these parents is not only a matter of what they feel as individuals. The very ability of a text like *Nappy Hair* to cause such an affront to dignity depends upon a set of discursive cues that are generally available. A scenario of misrecognition is not created, ex nihilo, by the individuals involved; rather, cues of misrecognition are hovering in the discursively thick air. It is precisely because of a long history of racial misrecognition that a white teacher's use of the *Nappy Hair* book can create the sort of moral affront that ensued in this case. Misrecognition is not only a vertical assault on one's "authentic" self, to borrow Taylor's term, it is also a lateral instantiation of misrecognitions that have happened over time.[15] To ignore the historically imbued progression of discourses is to pretend that the past never existed. It is to pretend that there have never been racist representations employed in the past.

This discursive understanding of the *Nappy Hair* encounter speaks precisely to the reasons educators cannot be satisfied, as were the media accounts of this incident, with a description of recognition that calls upon the intentions of the one-recognizing. Like it or not, the one-recognizing is part of a larger cultural conversation that began long before the recognitive encounter itself. As a teacher, I must own up to my own discursive position. As a white teacher, I cannot assume, because I have good intentions, that a long and continuing history of racist misrecognition can be wished away. I must be prepared to engage with others not with embarrassment or guilt about my own discursive involvement in misrecognition, but with a commitment to serious investigation of how previous discourses have positioned me within the encounter.

Unknowability

Coupled with such a discursive commitment, I find great insight in Martin Buber's reminder that the one-recognizing must be committed to a certain amount of ambiguity, a certain amount of not-being-able-to-know the other. I wish that I could convene my course once again in order to point out, to the preservice teachers who brought to my attention the *Nappy Hair* encounter, the following: Teachers need to be prepared to come up short when it comes to acknowledging their students, or to be prepared for coming up short of parents' expectations. Ms. Sherman's use of *Nappy Hair* turned out to be offensive to the parents in this case, but such a revelation should not be surprising. It is very likely that efforts to recognize individuals or groups of people will fail from time to time. Human beings are simply not that knowable, and it is a mistake to think that one will be able to know, ahead of time, how to proceed in any given recognitive scenario.

As Buber points out, a teacher must be a "great character." He or she must be ready to "react in accordance with the uniqueness of every situation which challenges him as an active person."[16] Whether it be because a student's cultural horizon is not well known to a teacher, or whether it be because an individual student is for some reason inscrutable to that teacher, educators must be prepared to meet the unexpected and unknowable recognitive challenges of a particular, unique situation. This recommendation may be uncomfortable for educators who are certainly used to being "experts" in their subject matters. As a teacher, I am used to knowing my material backwards and forwards. But when education is reconceptualized as a recognitive endeavor, then individuals are the subject matter just as much as mathematics or science or literature is. And individuals are often unknowable. It is a mistake to think that we, as educators, can ever have a person or a group of people down pat.

Subjection

I am disturbed that this recognitive encounter surrounding the *Nappy Hair* text did not turn out better, that the students were not given a chance to witness a recognitive give-and-take between their parents and their teacher, and that in the end there was only abandonment. Moreover, though, I am disturbed by the popular discourses that this incident set into motion, discourses that made it almost impossible in this struggle for recognition to appear valid in any way. In precisely the way that Judith Butler writes, this event is already circumscribed by a set of discourses that are already in play. Even as they try to enter a recognitive discussion, these parents are stepping into a position of subjection that undermines precisely the recognitive dimension of that discussion.

In the media account of this incident, and in discussions of the incident at large, as I have found in my own course with preservice teachers, the objections of these parents are couched within discourses of "educational-ese" that subvert the very message that the parents are trying to get across. For example, whereas the parents are trying to articulate a heartfelt insult, their concerns are met with educational discourses that have more to do with teacher effectiveness and literary merit than they have to do with the misrecognition that the parents intend to talk about. In essence, what the parents say is this: "We do not like the way that this text is mirroring our children's cultural identities." However, the discourses that are invoked around this complaint give answers that reinterpret the parents' objection. The parents' complaint is subjected to a more stereotypical assumption that "Oh, these parents are doubting the quality of the teacher or the text's literary merit." But the parents are not worried about Ms. Sherman's pedagogical efficacy nor about Ms. Herron's credentials; they are concerned that the text does not provide a positive mirror. Efficacy and literary merit do not speak to an affront to dignity. The parents' recognitive complaint becomes intelligible only within a set of discourses that subvert the complaint's recognitive dimensions.

Educators Need a Discourse of Recognition

This last observation, that the *Nappy Hair* incident ended up being couched in discourses that did not address the recognitive concerns of the parents, provides an appropriate spot for me to wrap up both this discussion on the *Nappy Hair* incident and this work. This story of Ms. Sherman and *Nappy Hair* was, as I mentioned, brought to my attention by preservice teachers who were struggling to make sense of what such an incident meant for their future careers. As I understand my students' reactions, most of them encountered the story with worry, mainly because their own educational lexicon did not speak to issues of recognition. My students' reactions to this incident were motivated by the same problem that plagued the seemingly irreconcilable positions of these parents vis-à-vis Ms. Sherman. A discourse of recognition is not widely available. It is difficult to get out of the either/or sorts of questions of intention and who has the high moral ground without a discourse that validates feelings of moral affront that result from an encounter with the other.

Such a discourse needs to be spoken by educators. The school personnel at PS 75 were, it seems, as ill equipped as my preservice teachers were to speak to an instance of misrecognition in the school. As I think back to why I could not articulate my own position to my students, I am convinced that I also lacked such a discourse of recognition. Ultimately, a discourse of recognition does not prove that either the parents were right or that Ms. Sherman was right. Such a discourse shows, instead, that the encounter needs to be a point of departure, not a breaking point. Who is right or wrong is not as important as that we create, out of a struggle for recognition, an educative moment.

In a case like the *Nappy Hair* incident, the parents, teachers, and students must engage with one another again and again, but not run away. An encounter like this should lead, at the very least, to the formation of a parent group that is consulted about the texts they would like to see used in the classroom. Parents and teachers should engage each other with their concerns and ideas about the merit of various texts. More, there should be an investigation into the interracial circumstances that laid the groundwork for this felt affront to dignity. Specific institutional changes can be made so that parents gain more positive institutional and interpersonal recognition at PS 75. Perhaps the preceding actions are not the particular steps that will work at PS 75; these are merely hypothetical consequences that might result from a project of social change within the school. My claim is not that a discourse of recognition offers specific institutional recommendations, it is rather that a recognitive discourse provides a way to begin talking about the necessity for such changes.

The task of this work has been to construct an educational discourse of recognition. It has been to offer a set of recognitive discourses "upon which we can ride," to go back to William James's pragmatic phrase. While the preceding analysis of the *Nappy Hair* incident is limited in scope to just one recognitive scenario, I am hopeful that the general themes laid out in this work are useful for thinking about, talking about, and acting upon in the many school circumstances where human recognition is at stake. Sometimes such recognition will be at stake in connection with the curriculum that we, as educators, ask our students to read. Recognition will be at stake in the ways that we confirm one another in the classroom, and in the ways that we offer students space to gather together to effect social change.

Moreover, recognition will be at stake in the ways that students treat one another in the public space of schools. There is a larger challenge that is implicit in the discourses of recognition that I have described in this work: to make these discourses widespread in education. It is a challenge to make recognition a subject that can be readily discussed, and readily acted upon, by all students and all personnel in the public space of the school. Our condition as beings who depend upon one another for a sense of dignity demands no less.

NOTES

1. This chapter thinks through a particular encounter in the sense that we will be doing an extended analysis of that encounter. But more, this culminating discussion is meant to emphasize a second sense of that phrase, namely, the importance of an encounterly way of thinking about the classroom. In this second sense,

we will be thinking, through the encounter, about schools. As I have shown in earlier chapters, recognition calls upon a set of discourses that help us to think profoundly about education and about the flourishing of students and teachers.

2. Carolivia Herron, *Nappy Hair* (New York: Knopf, 1997).

3. For my account of this encounter, I am relying on the popular texts listed below. Whether the facts are presented accurately by these periodicals is not my concern; what I am concerned about are the discourses that are available to educators in order to speak to incidents that resemble this sort of encounter. "Caught in the Cross-Fire," *Newsweek*, 14 December 1998, 38; Lynette Holloway, "After Objection to a Book, A Teacher Is Transferred," *New York Times*, 24 November 1998, 5; Lynette Holloway, "School Officials Support Teacher on Book That Parents Call Racially Insensitive," *New York Times*, 25 November 1998, 10; Lynette Holloway, "Teacher Threatened over Book Weighs Switching Schools," *New York Times*, 27 November 1998, 14; Jill Nelson, "Stumbling Upon a Race Secret," *New York Times*, 28 November 1998, 15; Lynette Holloway, "Threatened over Book, Teacher Leaves School," *New York Times*, 1 December 1998, 15; Clyde Haberman, "Cry Racism, and Watch Knees Jerk," *New York Times*, 4 December 1998, 6; Lynette Holloway, "Unswayed by Debate on Children's Book," *New York Times*, 10 December 1998, 3; "Fallout from the 'Nappy Hair' Furor," *New York Times*, 11 December 1998, 34; Lynette Holloway, "Crew Defends Teacher in Book Dispute," *New York Times*, 15 December 1998, 3.

4. Holloway, "School Officials," 10.

5. Holloway, "School Officials," 10.

6. Holloway, "Teacher Threatened," 14.

7. All quotations here from "Caught in the Cross-Fire."

8. Holloway, "School Officials," 10.

9. Holloway, "School Officials," 10.

10. Holloway, "Teacher Threatened," 14.

11. Holloway, "Teacher Threatened," 14.

12. Holloway, "Unswayed," 3.

13. Charles Taylor, "The Politics of Recognition," in *Multiculturalism: Examining the Politics of Recognition*, edited by Amy Gutman (Princeton, N.J.: Princeton University Press, 1994), 25.

14. Martin Buber, *Between Man and Man* (New York: Collier Books, 1965), 89.

15. Charles Taylor, *The Ethics of Authenticity* (Cambridge: Harvard University Press, 1991).

16. Buber, *Between Man and Man*, 113.

Bibliography

Althusser, Louis. "Ideology and Ideological State Apparatuses (Notes towards an Investigation)." In *Mapping Ideology*, edited by Slavoj Zizek. New York: Verso, 1994.

Ashbery, John. *Self-Portrait in a Convex Mirror: Poems*. New York: Penguin, 1976.

Banks, James A. "Multicultural Education and Curriculum Transformation." *Journal of Negro Education* 64 (1995): 390–400.

———. "Transformative Knowledge, Curriculum Reform, and Action." In *Multicultural Education, Transformative Knowledge, and Action: Historical and Contemporary Perspectives*, edited by James A. Banks. New York: Teachers College Press, 1996.

———. *An Introduction to Multicultural Education*. Boston: Allyn and Bacon, 1994.

Barber, Benjamin. *An Aristocracy of Everyone*. New York: Oxford University Press, 1992.

Benjamin, Jessica. *The Bonds of Love: Psychoanalysis, Feminism, and the Problem of Domination*. New York: Pantheon, 1988.

———. *Like Subjects, Love Objects: Essays on Recognition and Sexual Difference*. New Haven, Conn.: Yale University Press, 1995.

———. *Shadow of the Other: Intersubjectivity and Gender in Psychoanalysis*. New York: Routledge, 1998.

Bingham, Charles. "The Poetic Theorizing of Langston Hughes: Curriculum and Education of Identity." *Journal of Thought* 33 (1998): 15–26.

Bingham, Charles, and Kate Evans. "Tag You're It, Fag You're It: Theorizing Performativity in Education." Paper presented at the Journal of Curriculum Theorizing Conference, Lexington, Kentucky, 22 October 1998.

Britzman, Deborah P. *Lost Subjects, Contested Objects: Toward a Psychoanalytic Inquiry of Learning*. Albany: SUNY Press, 1999.

Britzman, Deborah P., and Alice J. Pitt. "Pedagogy and Transference: Casting the Past of Learning into the Presence of Teaching." *Theory into Practice* 35 (1996): 117–123.

Buber, Martin. *Knowledge of Man*. London: George Allen & Unwin, 1965.

———. *Between Man and Man*. New York: Collier Books, 1965.

———. *I and Thou*. New York: Charles Scribner's Sons, 1970.

Butler, Judith. *Subjects of Desire: Hegelian Reflections in Twentieth-Century France*. New York: Columbia University Press, 1987.

———. *Gender Trouble*. New York: Routledge, 1990.

———. "For a Careful Reading." In *Feminist Contentions: A Philosophical Exchange*, edited by Linda Nicholson. New York: Routledge, 1995.

———. *Excitable Speech: A Politics of the Performative*. New York: Routledge, 1997.

———. *The Psychic Life of Power*. Stanford, Calif.: Stanford University Press, 1997.

———. "Performative Acts and Gender Constitution: An Essay in Phenomenology and Feminist Theory." In *Writing on the Body: Female Embodiment and Feminist Theory*, edited by K. Conby, N. Median, and S. Stanbury. New York: Columbia University Press, 1998.

Campbell, James. *Understanding John Dewey*. Chicago: Open Court, 1995.

Cohen, Adir. *The Educational Philosophy of Martin Buber*. East Brunswick, N.J.: Associated University Presses, 1983.

Dewey, John. *Experience and Education*. New York: Collier Books, 1963.

———. *Democracy and Education*. New York: Free Press, 1966.

Ellsworth, Elizabeth. "Why Doesn't This Feel Empowering?" *Harvard Educational Review* 59 (1989): 297–324.

———. *Teaching Positions: Difference, Pedagogy, and the Power of Address*. New York: Teachers College Press, 1997.

Fanon, Franz. *Black Skins/White Masks*, translated by Charles Lam Markmann. New York: Grove Press, 1967.

Foucault, Michel. "Nietzsche, Genealogy, History." In *Michel Foucault: Language, Counter-Memory, Practice: Selected Essays and Interviews*, edited by D. F. Bouchard. New York: Cornell University Press, 1977.

———. *Discipline and Punish*. New York: Vintage, 1977.

———. *The History of Sexuality, Vol. I*. New York: Vintage, 1978.

———. *Power/Knowledge: Selected Interviews & Other Writings, 1972–1977*, edited by Colin Gordon. New York: Pantheon, 1980.

———. "What Is an Author?" In *The Foucault Reader*, edited by Paul Rabinow. New York: Pantheon, 1984.

———. *The Uses of Pleasure*. New York: Vintage, 1985.

———. *Technologies of the Self: A Seminar with Michel Foucault*, edited by Luther Martin, Huck Gutman, and Patrick Hutton. Amherst: University of Massachusetts Press, 1988.

Frankenberg, Ruth. *White Women, Race Matters: The Social Construction of Whiteness*. Minneapolis: University of Minnesota Press, 1993.

Fraser, Nancy. *Justice Interruptus: Critical Reflections on the "Postsocialist" Condition*. New York: Routledge, 1997.

Freire, Paulo. *Pedagogy of the Oppressed*. New York: Continuum, 1970.

Freud, Sigmund. "The Uncanny." In *The Standard Edition of the Complete Works of Sigmund Freud Vol. 17*, translated by James Strachey with Anna Freud, Alix Strachey, and Alan Tyson. London: Hogarth Press and the Institute of Psycho-Analysis, 1986.

Friedman, Maurice. *The Confirmation of Otherness: In Family, Community, and Society*. New York: Pilgrim Press, 1983.

———. *Martin Buber's Life and Work, The Middle Years 1923–1945*. New York: Dutton, 1983.

Gadamer, Hans-Georg. *Hegel's Dialectic: Five Hermeneutical Studies*, translated by Christopher P. Smith. New Haven, Conn.: Yale University Press, 1976.

———. *Philosophical Hermeneutics*, translated by David E. Linge. Berkeley: University of California Press, 1976.

———. *Truth and Method*. New York: Continuum, 1994.

———. *The Enigma of Health*, translated by Jason Gaiger and Nicholas Walker. Cambridge: Polity Press, 1996.

———. "On the Scope and Function of Hermeneutical Reflection." In *Hermeneutics and Modern Philosophy*, edited by Brice R. Wachterhauser. Albany: SUNY Press, 1986.

Gaines, Ernest J. *A Lesson before Dying*. New York: Knopf, 1993.

Gallagher, Shaun. *Hermeneutics and Education*. Albany: SUNY Press, 1992.

Gendzier, Irene. *Franz Fanon: A Critical Study*. New York: Pantheon, 1973.

Greene, Maxine. *The Dialectic of Freedom*. New York: Teachers College Press, 1988.

Haskins, James S. *Always Movin' On: The Life of Langston Hughes*. Newark, N.J.: African World Press, 1993.

Hegel, G. W. F. *Phenomenology of Spirit*, translated by A. V. Miller. New York: Oxford University Press, 1977.

———. *System of Ethical Life and First Philosophy of Spirit*, translated by H. S. Harris and T. M. Knox. Albany: SUNY Press, 1979.

Hirsch, E. D. *The Schools We Need and Why We Don't Have Them*. New York: Doubleday, 1996.

Holub, Robert C. *Jurgen Habermas: Critic in the Public Sphere*. New York: Routledge, 1991.

Honneth, Alex. *The Struggle for Recognition: The Moral Grammar of Social Conflicts*. (Cambridge: Polity Press, 1995).

Hughes, Langston. *Selected Poems*. New York: Vintage, 1959.

Hutchinson, Jaylynne N. *Students on the Margins: Education, Dignity, Stories*. Albany: SUNY Press, 1999.

Jagose, Annamarie. *Queer Theory: An Introduction*. New York: New York University Press, 1997.

James, William. *Essays on Pragmatism*. New York: Hafner, 1948.

Johnson, James Weldon. *The Autobiography of an Ex-Colored Man*. New York: Penguin, 1990.

Kerr, Donna. "Toward a Democratic Rhetoric of Schooling." In *The Public Purpose of Education and Schooling*, edited by John I. Goodlad and Timothy J. McMannon. San Francisco: Jossey-Bass, 1997.

Kissen, Rita M. *The Last Closet: The Real Lives of Lesbian and Gay Teachers*. Portsmouth, N.H.: Heinemann, 1996.

Kohl, Herbert. *"I Won't Learn From You," and Other Thoughts on Creative Maladjustment*. New York: New Press, 1994.

———. *Should We Burn Babar? Essays on Children's Literature and the Power of Stories*. New York: New Press, 1995.

La Belle, Jenijoy. *Herself Beheld: The Literature of the Looking Glass*. Ithaca, N.Y.: Cornell University Press, 1988.

Lacan, Jacques. "The Mirror Stage as Formative of the Function of the I as Revealed in Psychoanalytic Experience." In *Ecrits: A Selection*, translated by Alan Sheridan. New York: Norton, 1977.

Lee, Jonathan Scott. *Jacques Lacan*. Amherst: University of Massachusetts Press, 1990.

Locke, John. *A Letter Concerning Toleration*. Buffalo, N.Y.: Prometheus Books, 1990.

Marcuse, Herbert. "Repressive Tolerance." In *A Critique of Pure Tolerance*, edited by Robert Wolff, Barrington Moore Jr., and Herbert Marcuse. Boston: Beacon, 1965.

Martin, Jane Roland. *The Schoolhome: Rethinking Schools for Changing Families*. Cambridge: Harvard University Press, 1985).

McCarthy, Cameron. "After the Cannon." In *Race, Identity and Representation in Education*, edited by Cameron McCarthy and Warren Crichlow. New York: Routledge, 1993.

Mills, Patricia Jagentowicz. "Hegel and 'The Woman Question': Recognition and Intersubjectivity." In *The Sexism of Social and Political Theory: Women and Reproduction from Plato to Nietzsche*, edited by Lorrenne M. G. Clark and Lynda Lange. Toronto: University of Toronto Press, 1979.

Morrison, Toni. *Sula*. New York: Knopf, 1974.

Narayan, Uma. "Working Together Across Difference: Some Considerations on Emotions and Political Practice." *Hypatia* 3 (Summer 1988).

Noddings, Nell. *Caring: A Feminine Approach to Ethics & Moral Education*. Berkeley: University of California Press, 1984.

Paley, Vivian Gussin. *The Boy Who Would Be a Helicopter*. Cambridge: Harvard University Press, 1990.

———. *You Can't Say You Can't Play*. Cambridge: Harvard University Press, 1992.

Parker, Walter C. "Navigating the Unity/Diversity Tension in Education for Democracy." *The Social Studies* 88 (1997): 12–17.

———. "Democracy and Difference." *Theory and Research in Social Education* 25 (1997): 220–234.

Pignatelli, Frank. "What Can I Do? Foucault on Freedom and the Question of Teacher Agency." *Educational Theory* 43 (1993): 411–432.

Pitt, Alice J. "Fantasizing Women in the Women's Studies Classroom: Toward a Symptomatic Reading of Negation." *Journal of Curriculum Theorizing* 12 (1996): 32–40.

Probin, Ellspeth. *Outside Belongings.* New York: Routledge, 1996.

Quint, Sharon. *Schooling Homeless Children: A Working Model for America's Public Schools.* New York: Teachers College Press, 1994.

Ravjee, Neetha. "Critical Recognition, a Framework for Access: The Case of Engineering Education." Ph.D. dissertation, University of Washington, 1998. Abstract in *Dissertation Abstracts International* 59 (1998): 1943A–1944A.

Risser, James. *Hermeneutics and the Voice of the Other.* Albany: SUNY Press, 1997.

Rose, Mike. *Lives on the Boundary.* New York: Penguin, 1989.

Roudinesco, Elisabeth. *Jacques Lacan,* translated by Barbara Bray. New York: Columbia University Press, 1997.

Sedgwick, Eve Kosofski. *Epistemology of the Closet.* Berkeley: University of California Press, 1990.

———. "How to Bring Your Kids Up Gay." *Social-Text* 9 (1991): 18–27.

Singer, Peter. *Hegel.* New York: Oxford University Press, 1983.

Sleeter, Christine E. *Multicultural Education as Social Activism.* Albany: SUNY Press, 1996.

Stewart, John. *Language as Articulate Contact.* New York: SUNY Press, 1995.

Tatum, Beverly. "Talking about Race, Learning about Racism: The Application of Racial Identity Development Theory in the Classroom." *Harvard Educational Review* 62 (1992): 1–24.

———. *"Why Are All the Black Kids Sitting Together in the Cafeteria?" And Other Conversations About Race: A Psychologist Explains the Development of Racial Identity.* New York: Basic, 1997.

Taylor, Charles. *Hegel.* Cambridge: Cambridge University Press, 1975.

———. *The Ethics of Authenticity.* Cambridge: Harvard University Press, 1991.

———. "The Dialogical Self." In *The Interpretive Turn: Philosophy, Science, Culture,* edited by David Hiley, James Bohman, and Richard Shusterman. Ithaca, N.Y.: Cornell University Press, 1991.

———. "The Politics of Recognition." In *Multiculturalism: Examining the Politics of Recognition,* edited by Amy Gutman. Princeton, N.J.: Princeton University Press, 1994.

Wald, Priscilla. "Becoming 'Colored': The Self-Authorized Language of Difference in Zora Neale Hurston." *American Literary History* 2 (1990): 79–100.

Walzer, Michael. *On Toleration.* New Haven, Conn.: Yale University Press, 1997.

Williams, Patricia J. *The Alchemy of Race and Rights: Diary of a Law Professor.* Cambridge: Harvard University Press, 1991.

Williams, Robert. R. *Recognition: Fichte and Hegel on the Other.* Albany: SUNY Press, 1992.

———. *Hegel's Ethics of Recognition.* Berkeley: University of California Press, 1997.

Winnicott, D. W. *Playing and Reality.* New York: Routledge, 1971.

Young, Iris Marion. *Justice and the Politics of Difference.* Princeton, N.J.: Princeton University Press, 1990.

Young-Bruehl, Elizabeth. *The Anatomy of Prejudices.* Cambridge: Harvard University Press, 1996.

Zinn, Howard. *A People's History of the United States.* New York: Harper Perennial, 1995.

Index

About the Author

Charles Bingham was born and raised in Washington State. His experience with the school as a place for cultural change began when, as a second grader, he was part of a voluntary bussing program aimed at desegregating schools in Tacoma, Washington.

He began his teaching career in all-black schools under South Africa's loathsome apartheid regime, where he taught English and mathematics. He also taught in secondary schools in Washington State for eight years. Currently, he is assistant professor in the School of Education at DePaul University.